lonely planet

AF215171

POCKET
AMSTERDAM

Catherine Le Nevez

Contents

Top: A'DAM TOWER (p164)
Bottom: Westergas (p60)

Explore Amsterdam_31

Amsterdam Toolkit_173

FROM TOP: LEFT: MARTIJN KORT, VIA A'DAM TOWER; WESTERGAS

★ Top Experiences

Worth a Trip

The Journey Begins Here

Amsterdam's medieval core and canal ring are still startlingly recognisable in the 17th-century paintings hanging in galleries like the Rijksmuseum. Yet it's recently seen radical changes – not only the regeneration of industrial areas like Amsterdam Noord, or even the construction of entire neighbourhoods on newly created islands, but above all its reckoning with the role of colonisation in the city's history and prosperity, and its rapid uptake of sustainability strategies that include becoming a circular economy. In a sense, by drawing on its centuries of visionary ambition, determination and realisation, the city itself is coming full circle.

Catherine Le Nevez

lonelyplanet.com/authors/catherine-le-nevez
A Lonely Planet author since 2004, contributing to well over 100 guides in some two dozen countries, Catherine has a Doctorate of Creative Arts in Writing and insatiable wanderlust.

Canal cruise
FOOTAGECLIPS/SHUTTERSTOCK

THE BEST

Art Experiences

Amsterdam's world-class museums are packed with masterpieces from the Dutch Masters and later modern and contemporary luminaries, while art-in-the-making takes shape at *broedplaatsen* ('breeding grounds'). Everywhere you go, you'll find original and unexpected public art.

View masterworks like Rembrandt's *The Night Watch* and Vermeer's *The Milkmaid* at the nation's treasure chest, the incomparable and unmissable **Rijksmuseum** (p98).

Understand the tortured genius of Vincent van Gogh through the largest collection of his works, along with his personal letters, at the **Van Gogh Museum** (p102).

Immerse yourself in wild and wonderful modern and contemporary art at the

Stedelijk Museum (pictured above left; p110), its 21st-century 'bathtub' wing and its stunning 2025-opened sculpture hall.

Enter a Keizersgracht canal house to see anything from fashion retrospectives to travel photographers' storytelling at leading photo museum, **Foam** (p87).

Check out vibrantly coloured, often ephemeral creations in Noord's NDSM at the world's largest museum for graffiti and street art, **Straat** (pictured above right; p165).

Right: Van Gogh Museum (p102)

THE BEST

Architecture Experiences

Amsterdam's wealthy 17th-century merchants determined the city's look. Its lovely canalscapes were spared from wartime destruction, and the city has been careful to preserve its core, today edged by striking contemporary additions.

Stop by venerable church the **Oude Kerk** (p38), dating from 1306 in Gothic style and standing the test of time as Amsterdam's oldest surviving building.

Be wowed by the cupola and neo-Renaissance towers of the **Co-kathedrale Basiliek van de Heilige Nicolaas** (p42).

Admire the beautiful **Westerkerk** (p59), a Dutch Renaissance landmark on the Prinsengracht by city sculptor Hendrick de Keyser.

Discover a groundbreaking example of Amsterdamse School (Amsterdam School) architecture at the museum of housing complex **De Dageraad** (p127), part of HP Berlage's Plan Zuid.

See the rich interiors, coach house and hedged courtyard garden of the opulent 1672 residence that's now the **Museum Van Loon** (pictured above left; p82).

Glimpse future urban landscapes at Amsterdam Architecture Foundation, **Arcam** (pictured above right; p155).

Right: Co-kathedrale Basiliek van de Heilige Nicolaas (p42)

FROM LEFT: ZUMA PRESS/ALAMY, ATLANTIDE PHOTOTRAVEL/GETTY IMAGES, SMPOLY/SHUTTERSTOCK

THE BEST

History Experiences

Amsterdam teems with history. As the nation rethinks, re-examines and reckons with darker aspects over the centuries, momentum is building across museums to include a wider range of voices and tell richer, fuller stories.

Navigate seafaring history in the 1656 Admiralty of Amsterdam storehouse and replica galleon by national maritime museum **Het Scheepvaartmuseum** (pictured above left; p150).

Ponder cultural themes of race, ethnicity and identity and colonial impact, inheritance and legacy at the reinvented **Wereldmuseum** (World Museum; p136).

Peer at objects spanning 115,000-year-old mollusc shells to 1980s mobile phones unearthed during the north–south line's construction at **Below the Surface** (p44).

Dig into the **Stadsarchief** (Amsterdam City Archives; p86), home to over 50km of shelves containing records of the history of its citizens.

Reflect on the circumstances and actions undertaken in Nazi-occupied Amsterdam at the moving and inspiring **Verzetsmuseum** (Dutch Resistance Museum; pictured above right; p153).

See projection mapping of the city's evolution on a 200-sq-metre city model at **Amsterdam in Motion** (p61).

Right: Amsterdam in Motion (p61)

FROM LEFT: TWYCER, VIA HET SCHEEPVAARTMUSEUM; MIKE BINK, VIA VERZETSMUSEUM AMSTERDAM; JITSKE NAP, VIA AMSTERDAM IN MOTION

THE BEST

Park & Garden Experiences

Amsterdam's parks and gardens are great places to picnic, spot birdlife, catch markets and festivals, attend concerts and theatre performances, find kids' playgrounds and get active.

Unwind in Amsterdam's favourite green space, the **Vondelpark** (p106), a haven of manicured lawns, ponds with swans, sculptures, quaint cafes, footbridges and winding footpaths and cycleways.

Discover rare species at the 1638-established botanical garden **Hortus Botanicus** (pictured above left; p151), with a palm house, butterfly house and the world's first fully sustainable and climate-neutral greenhouse.

Experience Oost's almost-tropical green spaces including the wetlands of **Park Frankendael** (p140).

Trawl the Albert Cuypmarkt for picnic supplies and head to the undulating lawns and ponds of the **Sarphatipark** (pictured above right; p126) in De Pijp.

Climb through the treetops, visiting a working goat farm, boat on the waterways and more in sprawling forest **Amsterdamse Bos** (p122).

MARTIJN KORT; VIA A'DAM TOWER

PLAN YOUR TRIP

OUR PICKS

A'DAM Tower (p164)

THE BEST

Panoramic Experiences

Amsterdam's low-rise skyline means you don't have to head up to great heights for elevated views down over its web of canals, gabled buildings and church bell towers.

Strap into a six-seater giant swing sailing over the 100m-high edge of 1970s office block turned attraction-packed skyscraper **A'DAM Tower** (p164).

Climb the external staircase (or enter from the museum) to reach boat-shaped **NEMO** (p150) and its deck-like roof terrace for free city panoramas.

Scale 155 steps up the intimidating **Oudekerkstoren** (Oude Kerk

Tower; p39) to see all of Amsterdam laid out before you.

Sip on sky- and light-themed cocktails at 11th-floor bar **LuminAir** (p158). Head out to its terrace for some even more impressive 360-degree views of the city.

Browse department store **De Bijenkorf** (p42) before heading to its cafe-restaurant, which opens to a rooftop terrace overlooking the steeples.

13

THE BEST

Tulip Experiences

Bursting into a rainbow of colours, tulips are a springtime spectacle and Dutch emblem year-round, with fervour for the blooms stretching back to 17th-century Tulipmania.

Pre-empt the season on Nationale Tulpendag (National Tulip Day; third Saturday in January), when 200,000 tulips are planted on **Museumplein** (p110).

Book **Keukenhof** (pictured above left; p171) mid-March to mid-May for its opening season to see seven million bulbs bloom at 'the most beautiful spring garden in the world' in the Bollenstreek (Bulb Region).

Learn about the history of the tulip and speculative frenzy Tulipmania at the

Jordaan's delightful and illuminating **Amsterdam Tulip Museum** (p68).

Get up early to go behind the scenes of **Royal FloraHolland** (pictured above right; p128), where millions of blooms on thousands of flower carts are sorted for shipping worldwide.

Shop for bulbs and kitschy souvenirs (wooden tulips, fluffy clogs) at the **Bloemenmarkt** (p85), Amsterdam's once-floating flower market (now perched on piles).

Best for Kids

Perform hands-on experiments and engage in activities like designing your own wind turbine at the fantastic interactive **NEMO Science Museum** (p150).

Meet creatures great (like lions, elephants and giraffes) and small (such as non-poisonous poison dart frogs) at the historic and animal-friendly **Artis Zoo** (p150), and visit its neighbours, microbe museum Micropia and mind-boggling interactive nature museum Groote Museum.

Ride the miniature Amstel Train, get lost in the yew-hedge maze, play mini golf and much more in the **Amstelpark** (p128).

Visit the enchanting 100-room mansion for adorable felt mice (and sets for the children's artist/author's later books, including a mouse roller-coaster) at **Het Muizenhuis** (p45).

Descend to the large subterranean recreation site in Nieuwmarkt's **Vrog** (p150), offering streetwise activities from trick trampolining to parkours.

Best for Free

Attend free lunchtime concerts from 12.30pm on Wednesdays lasting half an hour at Amsterdam's premier concert hall, the **Concertgebouw** (p110).

Catch at least one free event a week, such as evening concerts, jam sessions or workshops, at the **Bimhuis** (p155), the jazz stage of the gleaming glass-and-steel concert hall Muziekgebouw.

Join hundreds of people stomping to high-BPM beats at long-running 'Techno Tuesday' at **Melkweg** (p88) – a rare free club event.

See uncut diamonds, watch diamond polishing in action and be dazzled by sparkling jewels at free and fascinating diamond factory **Gassan** (p152) in Nieuwmarkt.

Listen to the organs being played during free lunchtime concerts from 1pm to 1.30pm on Wednesdays at the Western Canal Ring's beautiful landmark church **Westerkerk** (p59).

Perfect Days

Amsterdam's compactness and efficient transport makes it easy to pack a lot in, but leave time for soaking up the city from *café* (pub) terraces and making serendipitous discoveries.

Melkweg (p88)

FROM LEFT: BEN HOUDIJK/SHUTTERSTOCK, COLORMAKER/SHUTTERSTOCK, HEINEKEN EXPERIENCE, WOLF-PHOTOGRAPHY/SHUTTERSTOCK

DAY ONE

Only Have One Day?

MORNING

Begin by viewing the masterpieces at one of Museumplein's three big museums: the mighty **Rijksmuseum** (pictured; p98), intimate **Van Gogh Museum** (p102), or modern and contemporary **Stedelijk Museum** (p110).

AFTERNOON

Explore the secret courtyard and gardens at the **Begijnhof** (p43) in the Medieval Centre. Stroll to the **Dam** (p42), where the **Royal Palace** (Koninklijk Paleis; p36) and **Nieuwe Kerk** (p42) provide a dose of Dutch history. In the Red Light District, the **Oude Kerk** (p38) has historical and art exhibitions.

EVENING

Sip *jenever* (traditional Dutch gin, p45) standing up like a local at **Wynand Fockink** (p45), and settle in for cocktails made from heritage Dutch recipes at **Dutch Courage** (p45).

■ DAY TWO ■

A Weekend Trip

MORNING

After brunch in De Pijp at a local hangout like **Bakers & Roasters** (p130), browse Amsterdam's largest street market, the **Albert Cuypmarkt** (p126). Then get shaken up, heated up and 'bottled' like a beer at the **Heineken Experience** (pictured; p120).

AFTERNOON

Cross into the Southern Canal Ring to check out the opulent canal-house lifestyle at **Museum Van Loon** (p82), edgy photography exhibitions at **Foam** (p87) and bulbs galore at the **Bloemenmarkt** (p85).

EVENING

After dark, par-tee at hyperactive, neon-lit **Leidseplein** (p88), surrounded by good-time clubs and *bruin cafés* (traditional Dutch pubs), and/or nearby **Rembrandtplein** (p88). **Paradiso** (p89) and **Melkweg** (p88) host the coolest agendas. Or catch atmospheric gigs at **Jazz Café Alto** (p89).

■ DAY THREE ■

A Short Break

MORNING

Take a spin around Amsterdam's beloved **Vondelpark** (pictured; p106). It's easy to explore on a morning jaunt – and all the better zipping by the ponds, gardens and sculptures on a bike.

AFTERNOON

Immerse yourself in the speciality shops of **Negen Straatjes** (p66). At the nearby **Anne Frank Huis** (p56), the claustrophobic rooms give an all-too-real feel for Anne's life in hiding, as does seeing her diary.

EVENING

Set sail with operators like **Pure Boats** (p67) to see the waterways illuminated at night. Spend the evening in the Jordaan, enjoying a glass on a canal-side terrace at **Café 't Smalle** (p73) or heaps of other *gezellig* (cosy) haunts.

If You Have More Time

Find out what's on while you're here, from festivals to concerts – check the programme for the city's celebrated venues such as the **Nationale Opera & Ballet** (p155), **Concertgebouw** (p110), **Muziekgebouw aan 't IJ** (p155) and jazz stage **Bimhuis** (p155).

More time lets you discover less touristed areas like **Westergas** (p60), a former gasworks and park now transformed into a 'cultural village'. Its 19th-century buildings now house art and digital museums including the world's largest multimedia city scale model at **Amsterdam in Motion** (p61), as well as diverse eating and drinking options including a fabulous brewery, **Brouwerij Troost** (p131).

Across the IJ, reached by free, five-minute ferries, Amsterdam Noord is rapidly gentrifying but you can still visit its derelict former shipyards turned artist hangouts at **NDSM** (p165), including street-art museum **Straat** (p165). Attraction-packed high-rise **A'DAM Tower** (p164) has some of the best views of Amsterdam's skyline. Noord borders green polder countryside; start exploring by cycling to bucolic covered market **Landmarkt** (p167).

Nationale Opera & Ballet (p155)

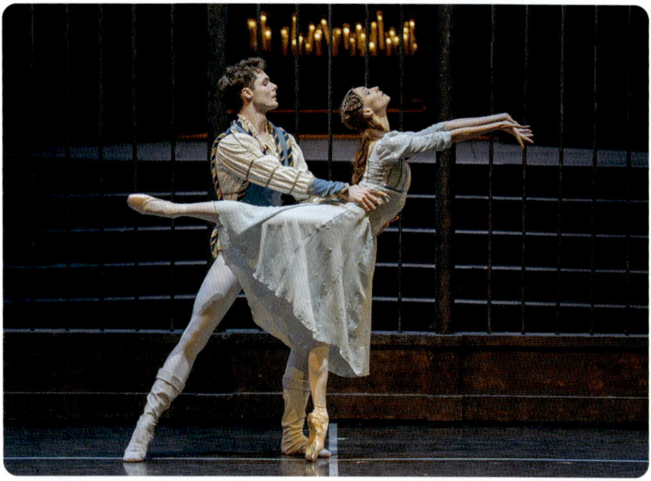

ALTIN KAFTIRA, VIA DUTCH NATIONAL OPERA & BALLET

A City Day Trip

On a Rainy Day

Amsterdam is on the doorstep of historic canal-laced cities, windmills and beaches, and bulb fields bursting with tulips. To experience all of the above in one easy-to-reach destination, take a quick 37-minute train trip to Leiden. Rembrandt was born and studied in this grand old city; you can retrace his early life on a walking trail, and see works in Leiden's splendid **Museum De Lakenhal** (pictured above left; p170). Also here is the nation's oldest and most prestigious university and a cache of museums.

Amsterdam's museums are ideal for rainy days. They include the old-world elegance of **Wereldmuseum Amsterdam** (p136), which addresses the Netherlands' colonial history and celebrates world cultures.

In the neighbouring Eastern Docklands, national maritime museum **Het Scheepvaartmuseum** (p150) powerfully reinterprets Dutch seafaring history. Nearby sights include Nieuwmarkt's historic **Joods Cultureel Kwartier** (Jewish Cultural Quarter; p153), the profound **Verzetsmuseum** (Dutch Resistance Museum; p153) or the steamy greenhouses of Plantage's **Hortus Botanicus** (p151).

From Leiden you can cycle through dunes and tulip fields, and view seven million colourful blooms at **Keukenhof** (p171) in season.

Cinephiles will love Amsterdam's wonderful array of cinemas, including its oldest, 1912-opened **The Movies** (p68), and the spectacular art-deco interiors of **Koninklijk Theater Tuschinski** (pictured above right; p87).

19

Get Prepared

BOOK AHEAD

Three months before
Book your accommo-
dation – Amsterdam's
hotels are in demand,
especially from spring
to autumn and on
weekends year-round.

Six weeks before
The Anne Frank Huis
releases tickets six
weeks ahead; many
other museums require
you to reserve a time
slot online.

One week before
Check the cultural
agenda on *iamsterdam.
com* to find concerts,
exhibitions, festivals
and events, and
book tickets.

Manners Matter

Respecting others is paramount; queue
jumping is frowned upon, as are blocking
pavements, making excess noise, litter-
ing and nuisance behaviour.

Punctuality is highly regarded;
tardiness is considered impolite.

The Dutch are renowned straight
talkers. Don't be offended if locals give
you their frank, unvarnished opinion.
It's not considered impolite, instead it
comes from the desire to be direct and
honest, and communicate clearly.

Spread Out

Amsterdam's Medieval Centre and
17th-century canal ring attract the
lion's share of visitors. Many never even
venture any further, but it's only a tiny
facet of the city. By exploring further, not
only will you help reduce overtourism
pressure on this small, tightly packed
area, you'll discover a mosaic of neighbourhoods home to great museums,
sprawling parks, forest and waterways,
unique shops, vibrant nightlife, and rich
and diverse local life.

Things to Know

Amsterdam isn't a 24-hour city; establishments keep regular hours, and public
transport is limited at night.

Fluent English is widely spoken
but using a few words of Dutch (eg
greetings) can enrich your trip.

Accommodation in older buildings
might not have air conditioning or lifts
(and staircases can be narrow and
steep). Bathrooms may be open-plan
or have limited screening (sometimes
even the toilets).

Of the Netherlands' 12 provinces,
Holland comprises just two: Noord-
Holland (North Holland; where Amsterdam, the national capital, is located)
and Zuid-Holland (home to cities such
as the second-largest, Rotterdam, and
Den Haag, the seat of government
and royalty). The country as a whole is
the Netherlands, not Holland, even if
tourism branding isn't always clear.

TIPPING

Tipping is customary but not obligatory.

 5% is fine; 10% generous

Restaurants and cocktail bars

 Not expected

Other bars and cafes

 Round to the nearest euro

Taxis

 A few euros for good service

Hotel staff

DAILY BUDGET

Budget: Less than €150

- Dorm bed in a hostel: **€20–80**
- SUP rental per hour: **€15**
- *Pannenkoeken* (Dutch pancakes): **€12.50**
- Bottle of beer: **€6**
- Live music gig: **free–€10**

Midrange: €300–450

- Double room in a midrange hotel: **€140–280**
- Two-course meal in a midrange restaurant: **€40**
- Boat rental per three hours: **from €90**
- Museum ticket: **€18**
- Glass of wine: **€8**

Top End: from €450

- Top end hotel room: **from €300**
- Fine-dining multicourse menu with wine pairings: **from €140**
- Private canal cruise: **from €150**
- Cocktail: **from €16**
- Concertgebouw ticket: **from €90**

Currency
Euro (€)

Language
Dutch (English widely spoken)

Time
Central European Time (GMT/UTC+ 1hr)

TATIANA POPOVA/SHUTTERSTOCK

PACKING TIPS

Notoriously fickle Dutch weather means there can be chilly spells even in summer. Bring a light trench coat or jacket (a proper heavy coat, woolly hat, scarf and gloves in winter) and an umbrella year-round.

📅 When to Go

Each season in Amsterdam has its own charms, from spring tulips to summer park picnics and canal boating, autumn festivals and winter *gezelligheid* (conviviality, cosiness).

Tulip season officially starts on Nationale Tulpendag (National Tulip Day; third Saturday in January), when Museumplein is carpeted with 200,000 tulips, but really comes to life from around mid-March to mid-May. As the weather warms up, the city fills with visitors throughout summer. From September/October, it's a fabulous time for photography as falling autumn leaves reveal the gabled canal houses. The city is quietest in winter (outside Christmas/New Year), but sights stay open, and museums and *bruin cafés* make wonderful refuges from the elements. Year-round, festivals abound.

Headline Festivals

April: Amsterdam's – and the nation's – biggest event is **Konings-dag** (King's Day), on King Willem-Alexander's birthday, 27 April (26 April if the 27th is a Sunday). Celebrations start the night before on **King's Night** (Koningsnacht); from 6am, the city becomes a sea of orange outfits and *vrijmarkt* ('flea market') stalls.

July/August: One of the world's LGBTIQ+ capitals, Amsterdam has over 500 events during the 15-day-long **Pride Amsterdam** (*pride. amsterdam*); the highlight is its Canal Parade, with 80 spectacular floats sailing through the city.

October: Massive five-day (and night) electronic music industry conference-and-festival **ADE** (Amsterdam Dance Event; *amsterdam-dance-event.nl*) has more than 1000 events at over 200 venues across the city.

Late November to Mid-January: Light-art displays illuminate the waterways (with app-based routes

Amsterdam

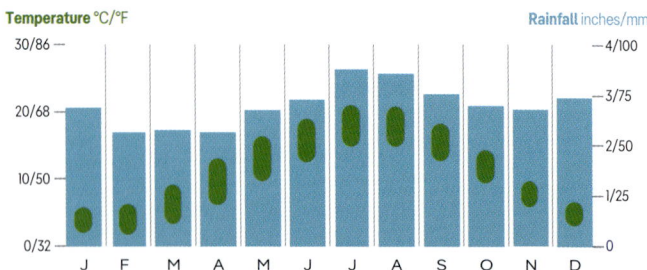

Temperature °C/°F — Rainfall inches/mm

	J	F	M	A	M	J	J	A	S	O	N	D

30/86

20/68

10/50

0/32

4/100

3/75

2/50

1/25

0

ANP/ALAMY

Keti Koti, Oosterpark (139)

and boat cruises) during the **Amsterdam Light Festival** *(amsterdamlightfestival.com)*, part of the magical Amsterdam Winter Festival.

Local Favourites

March/April: From Friday to Sunday over the Easter weekend, electronic music, art and sustainability festival **DGTL** (p165) at NDSM-werf in Amsterdam Noord runs on renewable energy and has plant-based food stalls

July: On 1 July, **Keti Koti**, meaning 'broken chains', has a parade from Waterlooplein to Oosterpark for the national commemoration of Dutch colonies' abolition of slavery, followed by a huge party on Museumplein with stalls sizzling up Surinamese BBQ and serving syrup-laced shaved ice.

August: Parks, squares, canal houses and floating stages on the picturesque *grachten* (city canals) themselves host concerts by talented young classical and jazz musicians during the 10-day **Grachten Festival** *(grachtenfestival.nl)*.

August: Open-air deck-chair cinema **Pluk de Nacht** (Seize the Night; *plukdenacht.nl*) screens independent arthouse, documentary, animation and short films (in English or with subtitles) over 10 summer evenings.

─── **ACCOMMODATION LOWDOWN** ───

Amsterdam's popularity means it no longer has a 'tourist season': book ahead year-round. With great transport and cycling infrastructure, staying beyond the historic centre can cost considerably less. Avoid private holiday rentals that contribute to Amsterdam's housing shortage (hotels can often work out cheaper).

✈ Getting There

Global hub Schiphol International Airport is located 18km southwest of the city centre, served by trains, buses and taxis. Trains serve destinations across Europe, including direct Eurostar services to London.

From the Airport to the City Centre

Train

Trains depart from Schiphol's station beneath the terminal (platform 3) for Amsterdam Centraal Station in the city centre. Up to eight NS trains (*ns.nl; €5.20*) leave per hour.

Bus

The Amsterdam Airport Express (*Connexxion bus 397/Niteliner N97; connexxion.nl; €6.50*) is handy for Museumplein, the Rijksmuseum and Leidseplein. Buses depart every 10 minutes (hourly at night) from bus stop B17 (to the right as you exit Schiphol Plaza). Buy tickets online or from the driver (card only).

Travel Cards

An Amsterdam Travel Ticket (*gvb. nl; 1/2/3 days €18/24/30*) is a paper chip card that allows unlimited public transport including to and from Schiphol Airport by train or Amsterdam Airport Express buses. You can purchase it at ticket machines and GVB service desks at the airport. The Amsterdam & Region Travel Ticket (*€21/31.50/40.50*) version includes nearby day trip destinations (such as Haarlem).

Taxis & Ride-Hailing Services

Taxis to the city centre are around 25 to 40 minutes and cost from €40 to €80. Only take official taxis, departing from stand A1 in front of Schiphol Plaza. Ride-hailing services (eg Uber and Bolt) may be cheaper; meet drivers at app pickup points E1 to E6 on Koepelstraat.

Other Points of Entry

Rail

Amsterdam Centraal Station has Eurostar services from London, Paris and Brussels; ICE services to Frankfurt; Nightjet services to Vienna; and European Sleeper services to Berlin (DSB Copenhagen services are expected in 2026). Amsterdam Zuid has international services from Brussels.

Buses

FlixBus, with stops across Europe, goes to both Sloterdijk and Bijlmer ArenA. Both are connected to Amsterdam Centraal Station. Sloterdijk is the terminus for European services by BlaBlaCar Bus, and Prague services by RegioJet.

Getting Around

With its picturesque canalscapes and famously flat terrain, the centre of Amsterdam is easily walkable, while the surrounding neighbourhoods are perfect for cycling. The city also has a superb public transport network of trams, buses and metros, as well as free ferries that cross the IJ River to Amsterdam Noord.

Walking

Busy streets and narrow lanes mean the city's central neighbourhoods are easiest to explore on foot, which also allows for serendipitous discoveries of the cosy *bruin cafés* (traditional pubs), restaurants and charming shops that make Amsterdam so special. Never walk in bike lanes (marked by white lines and bicycle symbols) and always look both ways before crossing them – for your safety and everyone else's.

Cycling

Bikes are more common than cars in Amsterdam and 42% of all journeys are on *fietsen* (bikes). Rental shops are everywhere. Prices per 24 hours range from €15 for 'coaster-brake' bikes and from €40 for electric bikes. Theft insurance *(standard/electric bikes from €5/10 per day)* is strongly advised. Choose a rental company that doesn't have branding to blend in.

An alternative to hiring a bicycle for a day is to use bike-hire apps with pay-per-minute plans such as **Donkey Republic** *(donkey.bike)*.

FROM LEFT: DUTCHMEN PHOTOGRAPHY/SHUTTERSTOCK, DUTCH_PHOTOS/SHUTTERSTOCK

— **ESSENTIAL APP** —

Amsterdam's public transport is run by GVB *(gvb.nl)*; its app incorporates the journey planner *9292.nl*.

Take care to ride in the red-paved bike lanes, and to watch out for tram tracks, pedestrians and other cyclists.

Tram

Most public transport within the city is on its distinctive blue-and-white trams. Many of the 15 lines converge on Amsterdam Centraal Station. The vehicles are fast, frequent and ubiquitous.

Bus

In areas with fewer trams, the gaps are filled by buses (all will be electric by 2030).

Metro

Amsterdam has five metro lines extending to the outer suburbs. They're mostly used by commuters; line M52 is handy for visitors, running from Amsterdam Noord via Centraal Station and Rokin (near Dam), Vijzelgracht (in the Southern Canal Ring), De Pijp, and Europaplein (in Zuid).

Ferry

Free passenger and bicycle ferries cross the IJ River to Amsterdam Noord. Most depart from the waterfront behind Centraal Station; line F3 to Buiksloterweg (the most popular for sightseeing in Amsterdam Noord) runs frequently during the day and more intermittently at night.

Taxi & Ride-Hailing

Taxis are not an efficient way to get around given Amsterdam's traffic and web of canals. Locals generally prefer ride-hailing services like Uber or Bolt.

Public Transport Essentials

OVpay

For one-off journeys, if you don't have a travel card, by using **OVpay** you can simply check in and out with your contactless debit or credit card, or phone. It's charged per kilometre plus a fixed base rate, and billed as a single transaction at the end of each day (no prior registration needed). You'll need to use the same card/payment method to both check in and out.

Day Tickets

GVB has day tickets and multiday ticket options (up to seven days), available as paper chip tickets or as barcode tickets within the GVB app.

Travel Cards

The **Amsterdam Travel Ticket** *(1/2/3 days €18/24/30)* is valid for unlimited travel by NS trains, the Connexxion Amsterdam Airport Express bus 397, and the Niteliner

N97 and unlimited access to all GVB trams, buses, night buses and metros.

A wider-ranging option is the **Amsterdam & Region Travel Ticket** *(1/2/3 days €21/31.50/40. 50)*, valid for unlimited travel by bus, tram, metro, and train in Amsterdam and the region with the operators GVB, NS trains, Connexxion buses, and regional EBS buses.

TRAVEL COSTS

Hourly ticket
1 hour €3.40, 1 night bus ride €5.60

Day ticket
1/2/3/4/5/6/7 days
€9.50/15.50/21.50/27/34/38.50/42.50

I amsterdam City Card
1/2/3/4/5 days
€65/90/110/125/135

USING TICKETS & TRAVEL CARDS

Day tickets and travel cards will be valid after checking in on your first journey.

ACCESSIBLE TRAVEL

Some trams have wide-opening doors and levelled platforms; those that don't will not be easy for those in wheelchairs. Check GVB *(gvb.nl/en/accessible-public-transport)* for wheelchair-friendly stops, use the GVB journey planner's accessibility option, or configure virtual stop assistance in the app. On board, all trams have designated space for wheelchairs and priority seating.

Accessible Travel Netherlands *(accessibletravel. nl)* and the Able Amsterdam *(ableamsterdam. com)* are good resources for further information.

LIVE TRANSPORT UPDATES

The GVB app's integrated journey planner calculates your most efficient journey options city- and countrywide, and provides live transport updates including crowd estimates.

🎁 A Few Surprises

You never know what you'll find in the worlds-within-worlds of Amsterdam's atmospheric lanes, charming canalscapes and creative neighbourhoods.

Waterway Explorations

In a city where a third of the surface area is water, it's no surprise that travelling on it is a popular pastime. There's no shortage of tourist cruises but for a local experience, hire a boat and glide past landmarks and out-of-the-way areas at your own pace.

Numerous places hire emission-free electric boats typically accommodating six or more passengers; you don't need a boat licence or experience. Amsterdam's first and oldest operator, **Canal Motorboats** (p67), has rentals from multiple locations and rents 'plastic fishing' equipment to clean up the canals.

It's also possible to get even closer to the water and explore the canals on guided tours such as kayaking through the Jordaan's charming canals with **Kayak in Amsterdam** (p67), or to hire an SUP from numerous places such as **SUP Tropisch** (p129) to paddle yourself.

Digital Discoveries

Today Amsterdam is at the cutting edge of tech, with a thriving start-up scene and groundbreaking projects from solar-panelled bike lanes to 3D-printed bridges. Museum and art exhibits showcasing digital creativity include Westergas' **Fabrique des Lumières** (p60), lifting both classical and modern art into a new dimension with over a hundred light projectors; the experiential series of rooms in a massive warehouse making up **AMAZE** (p71); and media-art hub **NXT Museum** (p168), where robotics, AI and VR are used in installations like data sculptures.

Green Dining

The Netherlands is a plant-based dining pioneer. A quarter of main meals eaten here are vegetarian and Amsterdam surpasses national averages: 60% of residents follow

---

OFFBEAT AMSTERDAM

Windsurf, wing-foil, wakeboard or flyboard at sandy urban beach **Strand IJburg** (p153), or play some beach volleyball or sand soccer.

Hoist a glass of beer at **Brouwerij 't IJ** (p152), a tiled former bathhouse turned microbrewery beneath the enormous sails of a 1725-built windmill.

Admire a grand canal-house art collection dedicated entirely to feline art in honour of the founder's cat at the **Katten-kabinet** (p87).

Kick back at off-grid **Café de Ceuvel** (p169), which is built out onto an island and made from recycled materials.

Proeflokaal A van Wees (p73)

flexitarian, pescatarian, vegetarian or vegan diets. It's on target for the municipality's goal of having 65% sustainable, plant-based choices available by 2030.

Vegetarians and vegans will find a plethora of options at all price points, from market-stall snacks to high-end gourmet dining. Many spots are exclusively vegetarian or completely vegan, and those that aren't usually have vegetarian (and often vegan) options available. The ultimate green dining experience is at **De Kas** (p141), inside the greenhouse that grew the ingredients on your plate.

Traditional Drinking

Around since the 16th century, *jenever* (traditional Dutch gin; pronounced ye-nay-ver, sometimes spelt *genever*) is more popular than ever. The city is home to historic distilleries and tasting rooms, such as **Wynand Fockink** (p45), dating from 1679, and **Proeflokaal A van Wees** (p73), pouring its Jordaan-produced house brands. New-generation cocktail bar **Dutch Courage** (p49) creates concoctions from 150 alcoholic varieties.

Alternative Entertainment

Longstanding counterculture history dating back to the city's 1960s/70s *magisch centrum* ('magic centre') era has given Amsterdam a stash of former squats that remain hotbeds of creativity such as **OT301**, **OCCII**, and former fallout shelter **Vondelbunker** (p111). The best place to find out about live, often alternative gigs and concerts is gig guide Hidden Agenda (*hiddenagenda.nl*).

Explore Amsterdam

Vondelpark (p106)
WOLF-PHOTOGRAPHY/SHUTTERSTOCK

31

See p47
for eating,
drinking and
shopping
listings

Explore

Researched by
Barbara Woolsey &
Catherine Le Nevez

Medieval Centre & the Red Light District

Amsterdam's oldest quarter is remarkably preserved. The Amstel's original mouth, Damrak, stretches south to the Royal Palace on the Dam, the site of the fishing settlement Aemstelredamme ('the dam built across the Amstel') that gave the city its name; its extension, Rokin, continues south to Muntplein. Side streets brim with 17th-century *jenever* (Dutch gin) tasting rooms, cosy *bruin cafés* (traditional pubs), boutiques and atmospheric restaurants. West is the shopping strip Kalverstraat. East, in the area known as De Wallen, are the narrow alleyways of the Red Light District, home to Amsterdam's oldest surviving building, Oude Kerk, and oldest canal, the 1385-dug Oudezijds Voorburgwal.

Getting Around

 **Walking**

Small, narrow streets mean this neigh-bourhood is most easily covered on foot. Ride-sharing vehicles aren't permitted throughout the centre; there's a designated pick-up point at Muntplein.

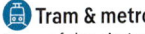 **Tram & metro**

Many of the city's tram lines go through the neighbourhood en route to Centraal Station. The metro travels from Centraal to Amsterdam's outer neighbourhoods, and to Amsterdam Noord and Station Zuid via Rokin in the Medieval Centre.

 Ferry

Free ferries to Amsterdam Noord depart from the piers behind Centraal Station.

★

THE BEST

PALACE
Royal Palace (p36)

CHURCH
Oude Kerk (p38)

ARCHAEOLOGY MUSEUM
Allard Pierson Museum (p43)

JENEVER TASTING HOUSE
Wynand Fockink (p45)

FRIES
Vleminckx (p47)

Munttoren (p41)
MILOS RUZICKA/SHUTTERSTOCK

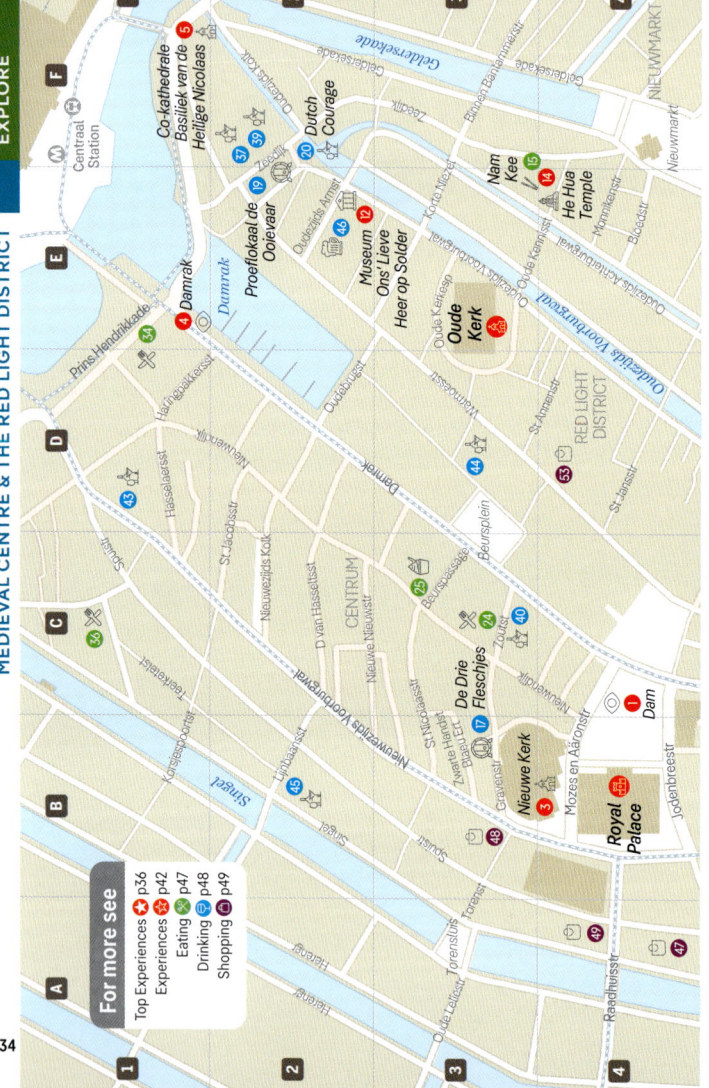

For more see

Top Experiences ✪ p36
Experiences ✪ p42
Eating ✖ p47
Drinking ⬤ p48
Shopping ⬤ p49

Co-kathedrale
Basiliek van de
Heilige Nicolaas

Dutch
Courage

Nam
Kee

He Hua
Temple

Proeflokaal de
Ooievaar

Museum
Ons' Lieve
Heer op Solder

Oude
Kerk

RED LIGHT
DISTRICT

Centraal
Station

Damrak

Prins Hendrikkade

Damrak

Oudezijds Voorburgwal

CENTRUM

De Drie
Fleschjes

Beursplein

Nieuwe Kerk

Dam

Royal
Palace

Mozes en Aäronstr

NIEUWMARKT

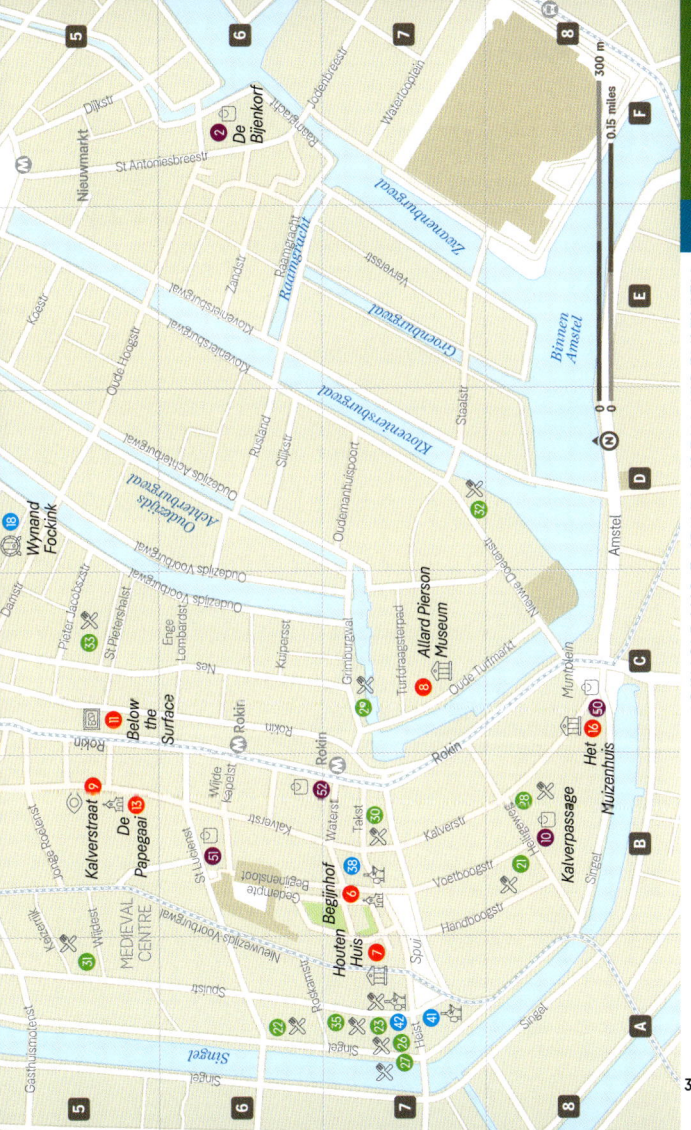

35

Royal Palace

The Koninklijk Paleis, Royal Palace, began life as a city hall and was completed in 1665. Its architect, Jacob van Campen, spared no expense to display Amsterdam's wealth in a way that rivalled the grandest European buildings of the day. The result is opulence on a big scale.

MAP P34 **B4**

PLANNING TIP

You can explore the monumental building if no events are scheduled; check the website's calendar for closures. Book tickets with a designated timeslot in advance online to ensure entry.

Scan this QR code for full opening hours and to book tickets.

History of the Building

French troops occupied the Netherlands in 1795 and in 1806, Napoleon installed his brother, Louis Bonaparte, as king of the Dutch Republic. Louis moved into the grandiose city hall in 1808, transforming it into a lavish regal abode.

After the French were overthrown in 1813–14 and William VI of Orange became Dutch King William I, it remained a royal palace, though never a permanent royal residence.

Like Dutch monarchs before him, King Willem-Alexander lives in Den Haag at Palace Huis ten Bosch, with Amsterdam's Royal Palace functioning as the royals' official reception palace. It plays a central role during state visits, holding gala state banquets and hosting heads of state overnight, and is the venue for other royal occasions including weddings, as well as award ceremonies like the Royal Award for Modern Painting.

Visiting the Palace

A self-guided tour with a free audio guide explaining everything in vivid detail takes around an hour. You also receive a copy of the booklet 'Traces of Slavery' shedding light on the building, which was partly financed from trade involving the exploitation and trafficking of people.

There are scavenger hunts for both younger and older children.

BENNING & GLADKOVA, VIA ROYAL PALACE AMSTERDAM

Palace Highlights

Most rooms are spread over the 1st floor, which is awash with chandeliers (51 in total), along with damasks, gilded clocks and some spectacular paintings by artists including Ferdinand Bol and Jacob de Wit.

The great burgerzaal (citizens' hall) at the heart of the building was envisioned as a schematic of the world, with Amsterdam as its centre. Check out the maps inlaid in the floor; they show the eastern and western hemispheres, with a 1654 celestial map in the middle. Sculptures here include a marble-carved Atlas holding up the sky (there's another cast in bronze on the palace's roof).

Louis Bonaparte left behind about 1000 pieces of Empire-style furniture and decorative artworks. As a result, the palace now holds one of the world's largest collections from the period.

Don't miss seeing the exterior at night, when the palace is dramatically floodlit.

TAKE A BREAK
Try the famed Dutch herring at teeny fish shop Rob Wigboldus Vishandel (p47). Sip *jenever* at 17th-century tasting room Wynand Fockink.

⭐ **TOP EXPERIENCE**

Oude Kerk

A historical and cultural treasure, Amsterdam's Oude Kerk dates back to 1306. Originally Catholic and now Protestant, the Gothic-style structure holds the city's oldest church bell, a stunning Vater-Müller organ and 15th-century choir stalls. The church was built to honour the city's patron saint, St Nicholas.

MAP P34 **E3**

PLANNING TIP
Visiting the Oude Kerk is quietest in the mornings on weekdays (especially Tuesdays and Wednesdays). Church services take place outside visiting hours on Sundays.

Scan this QR code for full opening hours and booking details.

History of the Church

Originally, this site was home to a graveyard built on a mound next to the Amstel River and wooden chapel constructed around 1213. A stone church replaced it in 1306 and it was consecrated in 1309 as the Catholic St Nicolaaskerk. It became known as the Oude Kerk (Old Church) once the **Nieuwe Kerk** (p42) was built in 1409.

The Oude Kerk's north and south transepts were added in the 15th century, and the Lady Chapel was completed in 1552. After Amsterdam's Catholic city council was deposed in 1578, the ransacked Oude Kerk went on to become a Protestant place of worship as part of the Dutch Reformed Church. Exhibits trace its long history.

Famous Graves

Many famous Amsterdammers are buried under the worn tombstones set in the floor, including Rembrandt's wife, Saskia van Uylenburgh (1612–42). Each year on 9 March at 8.39am, a beam of light touches her grave.

Other notable graves are those of diamond dealer Kiliaen van Rensselaer, naval hero Jacob van Heemskerck, organist Jan Pieterszoon Sweelinck and the family tomb of statesman Cornelis de Graeff, as well as Jacob Beeldsnyder, who had been enslaved. With wealthy families connected to, or involved with, slavery inscribed in its stained-glass windows and tombstones, the Oude

PIXELBISS/SHUTTERSTOCK

Kerk is reckoning with its past links to colonialism in the art exhibited here. Some 60,000 citizens lie beneath the church.

Visiting the Oude Kerk & Oudekerkstoren

Standout historical features include Amsterdam's oldest church bell (1450), 15th-century choir stalls with graphic misericords (wooden carvings) and Europe's largest medieval wooden vaulted ceiling.

Contemporary art exhibitions are a highlight. During concerts, you can hear the magnificent Vater-Müller organ (first built in 1726; rebuilt in 1742), 1965 transept organ, Italian organ and cabinet organ.

The Oude Kerk's tower, the Oudekerkstoren, rises 67m, reached by 155 steps; guided tours run from mid-May to October, hourly from 1pm on Wednesdays, Fridays and Saturdays, and from 1.30pm on Sundays. Buy tickets online or at the entrance (card only).

TAKE A BREAK
Attached to the church, **Koffie-schenkerij**, serving hot and cold drinks and lovely cakes, tarts and apple pie, has a sunny garden blooming with tulips in spring.

🚶 **WALKING TOUR**

Meander the Medieval Centre

History seems to seep from the brickwork on this walk through Amsterdam's Medieval Centre. Starting at a 17th-century tower where gold coins were once minted on the site of a 15th-century gate in the city walls, you'll wind past monumental buildings, plus surprises like immersive art and markets in secret passageways.

START	END	LENGTH
Munttoren	Magna Plaza	1.7km; 1hr

1 Mint Tower

The 35m-high **Munttoren** was first built in 1480 as a city-wall gate. Destroyed by fire in 1618, it was rebuilt in 1620 by Hendrick de Keyser with a four-faced clock; its 38-bell carillon arrived in 1668 (concerts take place at 2pm on Saturdays).

2 Lady Luck

Overlooking Rokin, Hildo Krop's 1948 bronze statue of a woman holding a ship's sail, **Vrouwe Fortuna** (Lady Luck) embodies the city's evolution from fishing village to global powerhouse. Moved here in 1972, it was stolen in 1989 but – as luck would have it – found again in a Belgian antique shop.

3 Secret Passage

A 17th-century almshouse, the **Oudemanhuispoort** is now part of the University of Amsterdam. Its passageway has an atmospheric secondhand book market and leads to a leafy hidden courtyard.

4 Historic Theatre Street

Once forming the Amstel's eastern riverbank, **Nes** was incorporated into the city in 1342. The Dutch East India Company (Vereenigde Oostindische Compagnie; VOC) was founded here at the home of merchant Dirck van Os in 1602, with theatres later lining the narrow street.

5 National Monument

Dam's 1956-installed **Nationaal Monument** commemorates WWII's fallen, who are honoured at a ceremony here on 4 May. Fronted by two lions, the obelisk's pedestal has statues symbolising war, peace and resistance.

6 Socially Minded Stock Exchange

Architect and ardent socialist HP Berlage's 1903 **Beurs van Berlage**, Amsterdam's financial exchange, venerates labour in tile murals of the proletariat of the past, present and future. Catch art exhibitions on its former trading floor.

7 Arcade Artwork

Chandeliers crafted from bicycle parts, stained-glass lamps, a shimmering fish fountain dispensing 'tolerance elixir' (water); and ship-wheel-and-anchor floor tiles enveloping 19th-century **De Beurspassage** illustrate how water formed life in Amsterdam in artists Arno Coenen, Iris Roskam and Hans van Bentem's work *Amsterdam Oersoep* (Amsterdam Primordial Soup, as the city's canal water is known).

8 Showstopping Shopping Mall

Amsterdam's spectacular 1899-completed former post office, designed by Cornelis Hendrik Peters in neo-Gothic and neo-Renaissance styles, was transformed in 1991 into **Magna Plaza**, with upmarket shops and restaurant-filled food hall beneath its soaring brick arches.

EXPERIENCES

See the City's Foundations SQUARE

Dam (MAP: ❶ P34 **C4**) is the very spot where Amsterdam was founded in the 13th century before it was granted toll-free status in 1275 and became a seafaring powerhouse. It's still a national gathering spot, and if there's a major speech or demonstration, it's held here.

The square was historically split into two sections: Vissersdam, a fish market where department store **De Bijenkorf** (MAP: ❷ P34 **F6**) now stands (head to its rooftop cafe for fabulous views), and Vijgendam, probably named for the figs and other exotic fruits unloaded from ships. Various markets and events have been held here through the ages, including executions – you can still see holes on the front of the Royal Palace (p36) where the wooden gallows were affixed.

Catch Exhibitions at the 'New' Church CHURCH

MAP: ❸ P34 **B4**

Consecrated in 1409, the late-Gothic **Nieuwe Kerk** (*nieuwe kerk.nl; adult/child from €7.50/ 6.25*) is only 'new' in relation to the Oude Kerk – the city's Old Church, built a century earlier. A magnificent carved oak chancel, a bronze choir screen, a 1645-installed pipe organ and enormous stained-glass windows dominate the spartan interior. It's also the site of royal investitures and weddings.

The building is otherwise used for exhibitions and concerts; check the agenda to see what's on when you visit. The annual photojournalism and documentary exhibition World Press Photo takes place here from mid-April to mid-September.

Visit the City's Cupola-Topped Co-Cathedral CHURCH

From the turreted 1889 Centraal Station and **Damrak**'s (MAP: ❹ P34 **E1**) canal-boat docks, the magnificent cupola and neo-Renaissance towers of the **Co-kathedrale Basiliek van de Heilige Nicolaas** (Co-cathedral Basilica of St Nicholas; MAP: ❺ P34 **F1** *nicolaas-parochie.nl/nicolaas; by donation*) dominate the skyline.

Named after the patron saint of seafarers (and the city), and completed in 1887, this was the first church to be built after Catholic worship became legal again in the 19th century. Its high altar and crown of Emperor Maximilian I are interior highlights. The church was elevated to a basilica minor in 2012, and elevated again by Pope Francis to a co-cathedral in 2025.

Sightseeing isn't permitted during services or on Sundays.

Step into a Serene Early-14th-Century Former Convent
COURTYARD

Amid central Amsterdam's cacophony is the pin-drop-quiet hidden *hof* (courtyard) of **Begijnhof** (MAP: **6** P35 **B7**). Dating from the early 14th century, this enclosed former convent is a peaceful haven, with tiny houses and postage-stamp gardens around the well-kept courtyard off of Gedempte Begijnensloot.

Within the courtyard is the charming 1671 Begijnhof Kapel, and the Engelse Kerk, built around 1392. The **Houten Huis** (MAP: **7** P35 **A7**), the Netherlands' oldest preserved wooden house, dates from around 1465.

Home to the Catholic order of Beguines – unmarried or widowed women who lived religiously without monastic vows – before the last died in 1971, today 105 women still reside here, so visitors must be respectful. This means no food, drink, smoking, photography of the houses, or any excessive noise.

Enter the convent via Gedempte Begijnensloot (the door on the Spui's north side is reserved for Begijnhof residents and church services).

Meet Mummies at the Allard Pierson Museum
MUSEUM

MAP: **8** P35 **C7**

Run by the University of Amsterdam and named for its first professor of archaeology, Allard Pierson

KALVERPASSAGE ART TOUR

Off high-street chain-store-lined **Kalverstraat** (MAP: **9** P34 **B5**), shopping mall **Kalverpassage** (MAP: **10** P34 **B8**; *kalverpassage.nl*) unassumingly doubles as a gallery with various statues and installations by international artists. QR codes beneath each artwork can be scanned for an Art Audio Tour revealing more about the artist and their inspiration. Each piece is also listed on the website so you know what you're looking for.

(1831–96), the **Allard Pierson Museum** (*allardpierson. nl; adult/child €15.50/3.50*) contains a rich collection of Mediterranean and Near Eastern archaeology. You'll find actual mummies (among them, a child, adult and animals), vases from ancient Greece and Mesopotamia, a very cool wagon from the royal tombs at Salamis (Cyprus), and galleries full of other items providing insight into daily life in ancient times.

With an extensive range of maps, atlases and nautical charts, its cartography collection is one of the world's largest. Like other Dutch institutions, since 2023, it has reviewed its collection to tell stories from lesser-heard perspectives, such as looking at maps and archives on Suriname up to its independence in 1975. This Surinamica Collection is now among its core archives.

Go Below the Surface

EXHIBITION

MAP: **11** P34 **C5**

With a valid metro ticket, descending to Rokin metro station opens up a window on Amsterdam's long history.

During the construction of Amsterdam's 2018-opened Noord/Zuidlijn (north–south metro line), more than 134,000 archaeological finds were unearthed from beneath the streets and waterways. Now 9500 of them dating as far back as 2400 BCE are displayed in glass cases between Rokin metro station's escalators at the exhibition **Below the Surface**. Transport, craft and industry, buildings and interiors feature at the southern entrance. Objects at the northern entrance span science, communications, weapons, armour, recreation, personal items and clothing.

Collection highlights include coins (from as early as 1371), ice-skating blades from the Middle Ages, 15th-century padlocks, 17th-century pottery, an 18th-century piggy bank, 19th-century pocket watches and military uniform buttons, a 1922 car radiator cap, 1935 toy car replica of the Bluebird that broke the world land-speed record the same year, and brick-sized mobile phones from the 1980s.

Seek Out Clandestine Churches

MUSEUM

On the Oudezijds Voorburgwal, what might look like a typical Amsterdam canal house outside contains an entire church. In the mid-1600s, when the Calvinist rulers had outlawed public Catholic worship, local merchant Jan Hartman built a covert church inside his home for his son to study to be a priest. Unexpectedly elaborate, **Museum Ons' Lieve Heer op Solder** (Our Dear Lord in the Attic; MAP: **12** P34 **E2**; *opsolder.nl; adult/child €16.95/7.50*) has a marble-columned altar, a painting by Jacob de Wit, a grand organ, and capacity for 150 worshippers. The building, with its maze of staircases, nooks, oak furniture and porcelain-tiled kitchen, provides a snapshot of 17th-century canal-house life.

An unexpected oasis in the sea of consumerism on busy shopping street Kalverstraat, the curious Petrus en Pauluskerk, aka **De Papegaai** (MAP: **13** P34 **B5**; *nicolaas-parochie.nl/papegaai; by donation*) is a Catholic church from the 17th century that was a clandestine house of worship, hidden in the garden behind a bird-trader's house. Note the *papegaai* (parrot) over the door.

Discover Amsterdam's Chinatown

AREA

Amsterdam's small, lively China-town centres around Zeedijk – constructed as 'sea dyke' to protect Amsterdam from the IJ River. It's the site of New Year celebrations (there's a lion dance on 2 January as well as Chinese New Year later in January or February). The Chinese community first settled here around 1911, with city authorities collaborating with its residents to breathe new life into the area from the mid-1980s onwards.

Built in 2000, **He Hua Temple** (MAP: 14 P34 E4; *ibps.nl; by donation*), Europe's largest Chinese Imperial-style Buddhist temple, is a shrine to Kuan Yin, the Bodhisattva (Buddhist goddess) of mercy. You'll see its classical roof carvings at Zeedijk 106–118; enter via the side gates.

Chinese grocery stores and restaurants congregate here; favourites include 1981-established **Nam Kee** (MAP: 15 P34 E3; *namkee. nl*) serving Cantonese classics like Peking duck.

Marvel at a Miniature 'Mouse Mansion'

MUSEUM

MAP: 16 P34 C8

An enchanting world in miniature, **Het Muizenhuis** (the Mouse Mansion; *themousemansion.com; free*) is the brainchild of artist/author Karina Schaapman, who crafted a 100-room home for adorable felt mice Sam, Julia and friend, then produced a series of children's books (22 to date) on

JENEVER TASTING HOUSES

The Medieval Centre has some fabulously atmospheric places to try the local firewater, *jenever* (p29), along with liqueurs.

De Drie Fleschjes

MAP: 17 P34 B3

A 1650 jewel with a wall of master-ship-builder-made barrels. *dedriefleschjes.nl*

Wynand Fockink

MAP: 18 P34 D5

Intimate tasting house (no seating) dating from 1679, with a house-speciality *boswandeling* (secret of the forest). *wynandfockink.nl*

Proeflokaal de Ooievaar

MAP: 19 P34 E2

Timber-lined tasting house not much bigger than a vat of *jenever*; deliberately built tilted in 1782. *proeflokaaldeooievaar.nl*

Dutch Courage

MAP: 20 P34 F2

New-generation place with 150 different types of *jenever* and old Dutch liqueurs. *dutchcourage cocktails.com*

their adventures. You can see the original mansion and sets for some of the later books (even a mouse roller-coaster) at this two-floor 'mini museum' and buy toys, books and materials to build your own mouse mansion.

RED LIGHT DISTRICT

In Amsterdam's medieval area of De Wallen (meaning 'the walls', for the original canal embankments here), the **Red Light District** dates back to the 1300s, when women carrying red lanterns greeted sailors near the port. Its sex-worker windows, strip clubs, fetish shops, 'smart shops' (selling natural hallucinogens), coffeeshops (cannabis-smoking cafes) and copious bars, especially on and around Oudezijds Voorburgwal and Oudezijds Achterburgwal, have made it a magnet for hedonistic (and simply curious) visitors. While the Netherlands is known for its tolerance and was the first European country to legalise all aspects of prostitution including brothels (in the year 2000), authorities have long sought to banish boisterous revellers and crime, and reclaim De Wallen's small streets and canals for residents.

A clean-up agenda set out in 2007 has accelerated post-pandemic. Having reduced the number of brothel windows, the city is endeavouring to shift activity out of the area altogether. A decision on whether to relocate the district's brothels by building a purpose-built, multistorey 'erotic centre' on Europaboulevard in Zuid (widely opposed by both residents and sex workers) will be made by the end of 2026. To date, guided tours past sex-worker windows have been outlawed, as has smoking cannabis in central Amsterdam's streets (banning tourists from coffeeshops remains under discussion; nonprofit centre **Cannabis College** *(cannabiscollege.com)* has information and advice). There are now earlier closing times for bars and clubs (1am midweek and 2am on weekends, with no admittance after 1am).

Meanwhile, city authorities have run 'anti-nuisance tourism' campaigns including a targeted 'stay away' campaign to actively discourage *feestbeesten* ('party animals'). Ultimately, the intention is for artists and independent businesses to move in to the area, and the expansion of cultural events such as mid-June's **Red Light Jazz Festival** *(redlightjazz.com)*, highlighting the longstanding jazz traditions of the district.

Best Places for...

 Budget Midrange Top End

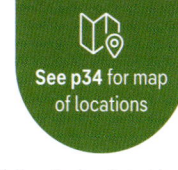
See p34 for map of locations

Eating

Snacks

Vleminckx
21 B8

Hailed as the city's best *friterie*, this longstanding kiosk offers crispy fries in traditional cones plus over 20 different sauces. *11am-7pm, to 8pm Thu*

Broodje Bert
22 A6

Canal-side sandwich shop named after its twist on the classic Dutch *broodje* (sandwich): house-special 'Broodje Bert' (lamb meat-balls on Turkish bread). *9am-5.30pm Tue-Sun*

Dutch Delicacy
23 A7

Dutch cheeses to savour on a cheese board or vacuum packed to go. Gouda-starring sandwiches as well as towering *appeltaart* (apple pie). *9am-7pm, from 10am Sun*

Rob Wigboldus Vishandel
24 C3

Tiny hole-in-the-wall fish shop serving excellent sandwiches with herring, Dutch prawns, fried whitefish and more briny delicacies. *8am-5pm*

Sweet Treats

Van der Linde
25 C3

A long line regularly snakes out the door of this narrow, generations-old shop where everyone is queuing for – wait for it – vanilla ice cream. Only one flavour but a whipped, velvety sugar cloud. *noon-5pm Wed, Thu & Sun, from 10am Fri & Sat*

Van Stapele Koekmakerij
26 A7

This bakery sells one thing: gooey dark-chocolate cookies with white chocolate inside made fresh almost hourly. Long queues (there's even a bakery 'bouncer') – wafting aromas are placating. *10am-6pm*

Lanskroon
27 A7

Famed for its signature take on *stroopwafels* (syrup wafers), with fillings such as caramel and espresso, honey and fig paste. In winter, follow the locals inside for homemade *speculaas* (spiced biscuits) and other Christmas treats.

Van Wonderen
28 B8

Instagram-approved *stroopwafels* with modern twists include *speculaas*, salted caramel, marshmallows and coconut. Buy one fresh – or a stack to take away. *8.30am-10pm*

Cafe Bites

De Laatste Kruimel
29 C7

Busy but homey vibes, with a canal-side terrace and vintage furniture, and even better baking (pies, quiches, cakes) and coffee. *8am-5pm Mon-Thu, to 6pm Fri-Sun*

Gartine
30 B7

Alley-tucked charm with mismatched antique tableware and organic-egg breakfasts. Come for high tea. *9.30am-4pm Wed-Sun*

Hummingbird
31 A5

Guest roasters and fair-trade beans focus in on the sipping experience; dishes include banana bread, cinnamon buns, cookies and croissants. *8.30am-5pm Mon-Fri, 9am-5.30pm Sat & Sun*

Café de Jaren
32 D7

Watch the Amstel float from the balcony and waterside terraces of this bright, spacious grand cafe. Coffee and lots of light bites. *10am-10pm Sun-Wed, to 11pm Thu-Sat*

Dutch Cuisine

Van Kerkwijk
33 C5

Low-key and easy to miss, but locals know: daily changing house special-ities of the finest Dutch fare. Tables are small and it's always packed. It doesn't take reservations and there's no menu. *11am-midnight*

Carstens Brasserie
34 E1

Skylit restaurant championing local suppliers within a 60km radius. Super-seasonal multi-course meals. Even wines from abroad have Dutch links. *6-9.30pm Thu-Sun*

D'Vijff Vlieghen
35 A7

Spread across five 17th-century canal houses, the 'Five Flies' is a vision of Delft Blue tiles and original Rembrandts.

Exquisite dishes – from smoked goose breast to roast veal and Dutch-crab mayonnaise. *5.30-10pm*

De Silveren Spiegel
36 C1

Elegant, old-world restaurant surrounds (step-gabled, 17th-century townhouse) and dishes (lobster stuffed with North Sea crab with vintage Gouda foam). Book ahead and dress to impress. *6.30-11.30pm Tue-Thu, 12.30-10pm Fri & Sat*

Drinking

Bruin Cafés

In 't Aepjen
37 F2

In one the city's last 15th-century wooden buildings, this quirky former inn was once frequented by sailors bar-tering *aapjes* (monkeys) for lodging. *2pm-1am Sun-Thu, to 3am Fri & Sat*

Café de Dokter
38 B7

Chandeliers, a birdcage and smooth jazz in a seventh-generation, family-run bar. *4pm-1am Wed-Sat*

De Roode Laars
39 F2

Shoemaker's shop turned lamp-lit, Dutch-liquor lair. *Jenever*, liqueurs and local beers – perfectly *gezellig* (cosy). *2pm-1am Sun-Thu, to 3am Fri & Sat*

Oporto
40 C3

Cool decor untouched in decades – woodwork zodiac signs, iron-framed parchment lighting. Play darts, down a glass. *11am-1am Sun-Thu, to 3am Fri & Sat*

Spui Terraces

Hoppe
41 A7

Filling glasses since 1670; crowds spill out from the dark interior onto the Spui. *9am-1pm Sun-Thu, to 2am Fri & Sat*

De Zwart
42 A7

Atmospheric interiors and a pavement terrace facing the Spui for *bruin*, beer and barflies. *10am-midnight Mon-Wed, 10am-1am Thu-Sat, 11am-8pm Sun*

Cocktails

Super Lyan
43 D1

Classy bar blending mid-century design with neon, futuristic vibes. Many cocktails have a tropical touch; try the

Surinamese Fizz (with pandan and cassava). *5pm-midnight Wed & Sun, 5pm-1am Thu-Sat*

Cut Throat
 44 D3

A men's barbershop, cocktail bar and brunch joint all in one. Sun-kissed daytime drinking includes margs and other tropical cocktails. *11pm-1am Sun-Thu, to 3am Fri & Sat*

Dutch Courage
 20 F2

Jenever and old Dutch liqueurs give the mixology here a heritage twist. The bar's name comes from when Dutch soldiers took a stiff drink of *jenever* pre-battle (strong cocktails here carry the tradition). *5pm-1am Sun-Thu, 3pm-3am Fri & Sat*

Tales & Spirits
45 B2

Beneath glittering chandeliers, sip decadent creations made with house infusions, syrups and vinegar-based shrubs. Vintage and one-of-a-kind glasses amp up aesthetics (menus keep what exactly is coming a surprise). *5.30pm-1am Tue-Sat*

Brewery

Brouwerij De Prael
 46 E2

Craft beers made with inclusivity: this socially minded brewery is known for employing the differently abled. *noon-midnight Tue-Sun, from 2pm Mon*

Shopping

Design

X Bank
47 A4

In a former bank, showcasing fashion, furniture, art, gadgets and homewares by established and emerging Dutch designers, and hosting exhibitions, workshops and launches. *10am-6pm Mon-Sat, noon-5pm Sun*

Mark Raven Amsterdam Art
48 B3

Artist Mark Raven's distinctive vision of Amsterdam is available on posters, coasters, fridge magnets and well-cut T-shirts that make great souvenirs. *10.30am-6pm*

By Popular Demand
 49 A4

Nifty gift-y wares, Amsterdam-inspired and (mostly) easy to transport – windmill or bicycle lapel pins and rock-'n'-roll Delftware. *10am-7pm Mon-Sat, from 11am Sun*

Quirky Shops

Andries de Jong BV
 50 C8

Serving sailors since 1787 with bells, bottled boats and other maritime gifts. Flags are quite affordable. *appointment only*

Posthumus
51 B6

This 1865-established, preserved-timber shop sells everything stamp-related – lacquer and rubber stamps, wax and ink – in Dutch-themed designs. *10am-5.30pm Tue-Fri, from 11am Sat*

PGC Hajenius
52 B6

The Dutch royal family frequents this tobacco emporium. Cuban cigars sold in gilded-and-marbled interiors and a smoking lounge. *9.30am-6pm Tue-Sat, noon-5pm Sun, to 6pm Mon*

Condomerie het Gulden Vlies
 53 D4

Condoms sold in every imaginable design to promote safe sex in the Red Light District. No photos allowed inside. *11am-6pm Mon-Wed, to 9pm Thu-Sat, 1-5pm Sun*

🚶 **WALKING TOUR**

Amble Amsterdam's Beautiful Bridges

Water makes up more than a third of Amsterdam's surface area. Threading through the city, upwards of 165 canals that help drain the landscape flow across 75km. They're spanned by some 2069 public road, cycle and pedestrian bridges – more than any other city in the world. This walk showcases some of the city's most beautiful.

START	END	LENGTH
Groenburgwal (metro Rokin)	De Ysbreeker (metro Weesperplein)	2.5km; 2hr

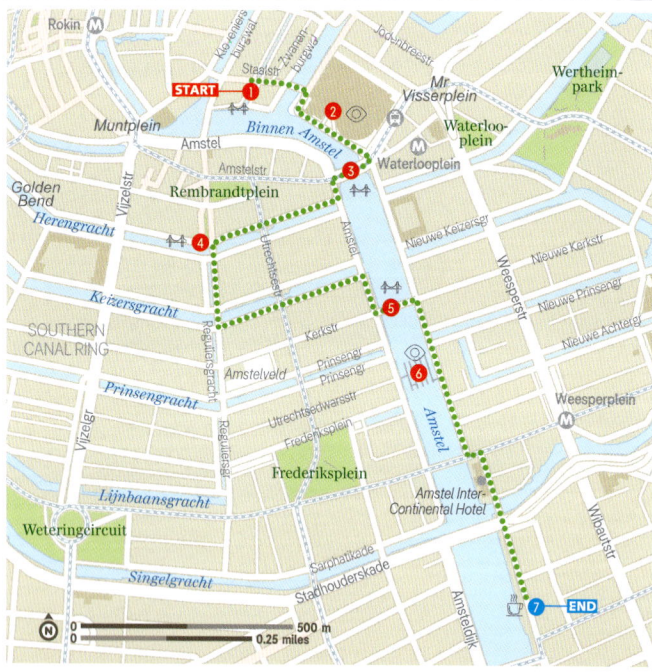

1 Impressionist Painting View

Step out onto the Staalmeesters-brug, the white drawbridge that crosses the **Groenburgwal**, and look north. Many Amsterdammers swear this is the loveliest canal view of all – a pick backed by Impressionist Claude Monet, who painted it in 1874 as *The Zuider-kerk (South Church) Amsterdam: Looking up the Groenburgwal.*

2 Amstel Views

Head to the curved, waterside building known as the **Stop-era** because it houses both the stadhuis (city hall) and the opera and ballet hall, aka the Nationale Opera & Ballet (Dutch National Opera & Ballet). Its terrace is a great place for watching the boats on the Amstel.

3 Blue Bridge

Cross the river via the 1884 **Blau-wbrug** (Blue Bridge). Inspired by Paris' Alexander III Bridge, it features tall, ornate street lamps topped by the imperial crown of Amsterdam, fish sculptures and foundations shaped like a medieval ship's prow.

4 Seven Bridges

Walk along the Herengracht to **Reguliersgracht**, the 'seven bridges' canal. Stand with your back to the Thorbeckeplein and the Herengracht directly in front of you and lean over the bridge to see seven humpbacked arches leading down the canal straight ahead. When they're illuminated at night it's possible to count 15 bridges in all directions.

5 Skinny Bridge

Walk along the Keizersgracht and cross the wedding photo favourite (and star of films including the 1971 James Bond thriller *Diamonds Are Forever*), **Magere Brug** (Skinny Bridge). It has a hand-operated central section that can be raised to let boats through. The bridge is especially pretty at night, when it glows with 1200 tiny lights.

6 Seventeenth-Century Locks

Continue south to the **Amstelsluizen**. These impressive locks, dating from 1674, allow the canals to be flushed with fresh water. The sluices on the city's west side are left open as the stagnant water is pumped out to sea.

7 The Icebreaker

Take Prof Tulpplein past the InterContinental Hotel to **De Ysbreeker**. Dating from 1702, it's named after a vessel that docked in front to break the ice on the river during the winter months (stained-glass windows illustrate the scene). Grab a seat on the enormous waterfront terrace to see what's gliding by these days.

See p72
for eating,
drinking and
shopping
listings

Explore

Researched by
Catherine Le Nevez

Jordaan & Western Canal Ring

Like scenes straight out of 17th-century paintings, some of the city's loveliest canalscapes and gabled canal houses are just west of the Medieval Centre in the Western Canal Ring. By the Westerkerk, the Anne Frank Huis, where the young diarist hid with her family in the Secret Annexe during WWII, is the area's main draw. Across the Prinsengracht, the Jordaan's tiny lanes, *bruin cafés* ('brown bars', ie traditional pubs) and vibrant street markets evoke its heritage as a former *volksbuurt* (workers' quarter) and are wonderful to wander. New developments extend in some of Amsterdam's most up-and-coming areas to its northwest.

Getting Around

 Cycling
Cycling is ideal in the more spread-out northern Jordaan and West; the Western Canal Ring and southern Jordaan's narrow streets are best explored on foot.

 Tram
Both the Western Canal Ring and southern Jordaan can be reached by tram (lines 2, 12 and 17) from Centraal Station; trams travelling along the Jordaan's western edge (5, 7 and 13) don't go to Centraal. Check for re-routings during municipal project 'Oranje Loper' *(gvb.nl/en/oranje-loper)*.

 Bus
Buses are handy for the northern Jordaan and beyond.

Canal with view of Westerkerk (p59)
S.BORISOV/SHUTTERSTOCK

THE BEST

HISTORY LESSON
Anne Frank Huis (p56)

SHOPPING AREA
Negen Straatjes (p66)

CHURCH
Westerkerk (p59)

CANAL MUSEUM
Grachtenmuseum (p66)

CULTURAL VILLAGE
Westergas (p60)

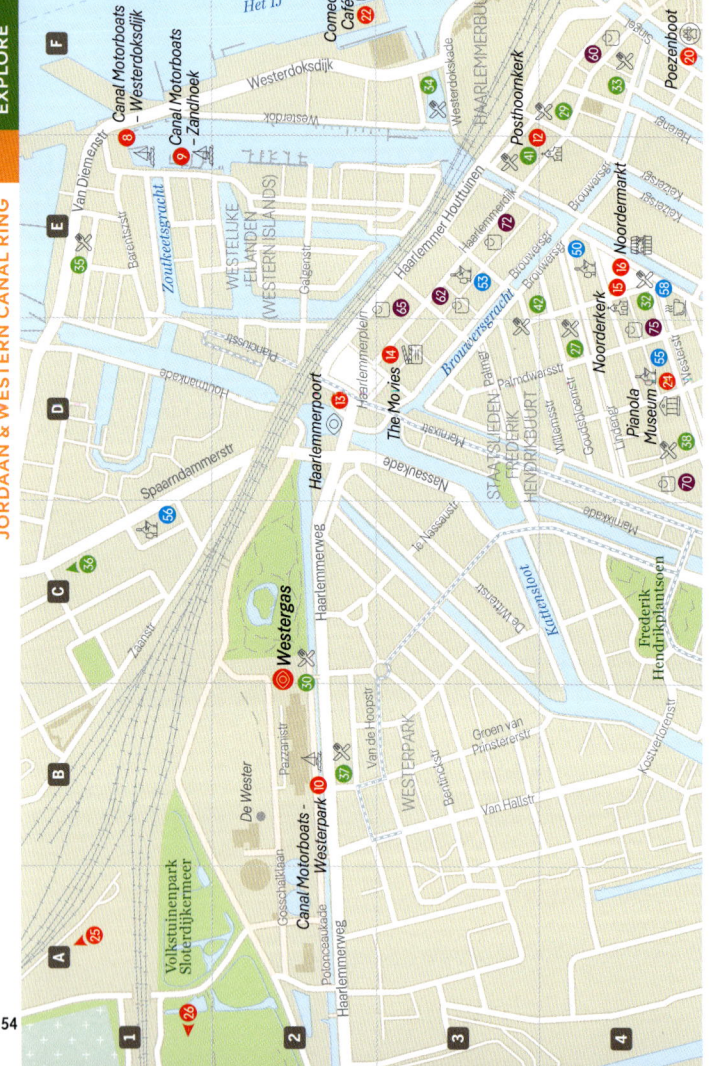

Het IJ

Comedy
Café 22

Westerdoksdijk

8 Canal Motorboats
– Westerdoksdijk

9 Canal Motorboats
– Zandhoek

34

Westerdoksdijk

Westerdok

60

Poezenboot
20

Posthoornkerk

29

12

41

HAARLEMMERBUURT

WESTELIJKE
EILANDEN
(WESTERN ISLANDS)

Zoutkeetsgracht

Van Diemenstr

Barentszstr

Galgenstr

Haarlemmer Houttuinen

Haarlemmerdijk

72

Noordermarkt

53

Brouwersgracht

82

65

Houtmankade

Planciusstr

14

13

The Movies

Haarlemmerplein

Haarlemmerpoort

Marnixstr

Nassaukade

1e Nassaustr

De Wittenstr

Kattenslot

STAATSLIEDEN
FREDERIK
HENDRIKBUURT

Palmgr

Palmdwarsstr

Villastraat

Goudsbloemstr

Lindengr

Noorderkerk

27

47

50

Bloemgr

Bloemgr

Bloemgr

Bouwerstr

Kostverlorenstr

15 16

32

58

75

24

55

70

Pianola
Museum

59

Frederik
Hendrikplantsoen

Frederik
Hendrikstr

Groen van
Prinstererstr

Van Hallstr

WESTERPARK

Beltstr

Van de Hoopstr

Westergas

50

Passanistr

De Wester

Gosschalklaan

Polonceaukade

Haarlemmerweg

Canal Motorboats –
Westerpark 10

37

56

35

Haarlemmerweg

Zaanstr

Spaarndammerstr

Haarlemmerweg

Volkstuinenpark
Sloterdijkermeer

25

26

54

CENTRUM

JORDAAN

MEDIEVAL
CENTRE

WESTERN
CANAL
RING

OUD WEST

DE BAARSJES

Miss G's
Brunch Boat

Pure
Boats

Anne
Frank Huis

Westerkerk

Antonia

Keesiedive

Grachtenmuseum
Amsterdam

Huis
Marseille

Negen
Straatjes

Houseboat
Museum

Amsterdam Tulip
Museum

Boom
Chicago

Johnny
Jordaanplein

De Nieuwe
Anita

Singel

Singel

Singelgracht

Nassaukade

Kostverlorenvaart

s105

480 m
0.25 miles

For more see

Top Experiences p56
Experiences p66
Eating p72
Drinking p73
Shopping p74

⭐ **TOP EXPERIENCE**

Anne Frank Huis

Heartbreaking and profoundly significant, the Anne Frank Huis is where young Jewish girl Anne kept a diary while she and her family lived in hiding from the Nazis in a Secret Annexe of her father's business premises for over two years until they were betrayed.

MAP P54 **D5**

PLANNING TIP
Timeslot-entry tickets are released on the museum's website at 10am on Tuesdays for visits six weeks later. No changes or refunds are possible. Beware of scam websites and scalpers.

Scan this QR code for full opening hours and to book tickets.

Build-Up to War

Anne Frank was born in Frankfurt, Germany, in 1929. Together with her older sister Margot and parents Otto and Edith, the family fled when Hitler came to power in 1933, settling in Amsterdam, where Otto Frank founded companies selling foodstuffs in offices and warehouses on Amsterdam's Prinsengracht.

It took Hitler's forces a mere five days to occupy the Netherlands, Belgium and much of France in 1940. Anne's diary describes how restrictions were gradually imposed on Dutch Jews: from being forbidden to ride streetcars to being forced to hand over their bicycles and not being allowed to visit Christian friends. Many Jews went into hiding. Otto and his colleague Hermann van Pels prepared a hidden Secret Annexe of Otto's business in spring 1942.

Life in Hiding

In June 1942, Anne received her red plaid-covered diary for her 13th birthday. The following month, when 16-year-old Margot was summoned to Nazi Germany, the family took shelter in the hideout. Soon joining them were Hermann van Pels, his wife Auguste and their son Peter (called the Van Daans in Anne's diary), followed by dentist Fritz Pfeffer (called Mr Dussel in the diary). The

CRIS TOALA OLIVARES, VIA ANNE FRANK HOUSE

household of eight lived with blacked-out windows in total daytime silence to avoid detection, and Anne's diary was the outlet for her fears and future ambitions. They were tragically cut short when the Gestapo arrived in August 1944 after the hiders were mysteriously betrayed. All eight of them were deported.

Anne died in the Bergen-Belsen concentration camp in March 1945 just weeks before its liberation, aged only 15. Her diary was found in the deserted annexe, and published in 1947 by her father, Otto, the sole survivor. Millions of copies, translated into more than 70 languages, have since been sold worldwide.

At the Anne Frank Huis

Accessed from Westermarkt, the Anne Frank Huis is contained within a modern, box-like shell

TAKE A BREAK
The museum has a cafe for quiet contemplation. In the surrounding streets there are numerous places to dine; for elegant vegan menus, head to Bonboon (p73).

POWERFUL DETAILS

The smallest, most moving details include the film magazines Victor Kugler bought for Anne, displayed in his office; Anne's treasured children's tea set that she left with her next-door neighbour Toosje Kupers before going into hiding; and, in Anne's parents' bedroom, the markings charting their daughters' heights – Anne grew over 13cm while living in the Secret Annexe.

that retains the building's original industrial character. Its museum shows multilingual news reels of WWII footage narrated using excerpts from Anne's diary. Temporary exhibitions also take place here.

You can see the former offices of Victor Kugler, Otto Frank's business partner, and office workers Miep Gies, Bep Voskuijl and Johannes Kleiman, who provided food, clothing, school supplies and other goods – often bought on the black market or with ration cards – for the hiders.

Above the office kitchen in the *achterhuis* (rear house), beyond the bookcase (pictured previous page) that ingeniously swings open on hinges, entering the Annexe's stark former living quarters is to step back into 1942. At Otto's request, the annexe remains unfurnished, but Anne's pictures of Hollywood stars and Dutch royals remain where she glued them on the walls of her small bedroom, which she shared with Fritz Pfeffer. When the museum opened in 1960, Otto had models made of the house that preserve the cramped, concealed layout.

After visiting the annexe, view more poignant exhibits including Anne's original red-checked diary, alone in a glass case.

Preparing to Visit

The museum shop stocks copies of Anne's diary and historic books but reading the diary before visiting makes being here all the more vivid.

Capacity is limited; arrive early for your pre-booked timeslot; afterwards, you can spend as long as needed; most visits last around an hour. Evenings tend to be the quietest time to visit. Admission includes multilingual audioguides.

When booking, it's worth adding on a 30-minute 'introductory programme' (in English; not suitable for under 10s), providing context on the house, WWII and Jewish persecution.

Be aware that photography is not permitted, and that there are a number of steep stairs.

Westerkerk

The Westerkerk (western church) and its bell tower, the Westertoren (western tower) are beloved by Amsterdammers; Anne Frank recounts its chimes in her diary, former Queen Beatrix was married here, and it's immortalised in songs, paintings and photographs. As low-rise Amsterdam's tallest church tower, it's a beacon across the city.

MAP P54 **D6**

The Church

Built in Dutch Renaissance style to designs by architect Hendrick de Keyser (1565–1621), who died a year after construction began, and completed by his son, architect Pieter de Keyser and city mason Cornelis Dankers de Rij, Westerkerk, the Netherlands' first Protestant church, was consecrated in 1631 and is the focal point for Amsterdam's Dutch Reformed community. Its barrel-vaulted nave is the Netherlands' largest. The main organ, with decorated panels, dates from 1686, and the choir organ from 1963.

After Rembrandt died bankrupt in 1669 at nearby Rozengracht, he was buried here in an unidentified pauper's grave. Look for the commemorative wall plaque in the north aisle. Among other Amsterdammers buried here are painter Govert Flinck and cartographer Joan Blaeu

See the online agenda for performances such as Bach night concertos by candlelight.

The Tower

The Westertoren was completed in 1638. Rising 85m high (87m including its weathervane), it's topped by the blue imperial crown bestowed for the city's coat of arms by Habsburg emperor Maximilian I in 1489.

Climbing the tower to the first balcony for panoramic views was unavailable at the time of research due to restoration works – check for updates.

PLANNING TIP
The 50-bell carillon rings out across the neighbourhood; recitals typically take place noon to 1pm Tuesdays. Hear the organs during free lunchtime concerts from 1pm to 1.30pm Wednesdays.

Scan this QR code for full opening hours and details of visiting.

⭐ **TOP EXPERIENCE**

Westergas

Ignite your creativity at Westergas, a former gasworks just to the northwest of the Jordaan, which has been repurposed in recent years into a cultural village with a growing collection of art museums and venues, as well as places for drinking, dining, clubbing and entertainment.

MAP P54 **C3**

PLANNING TIP
The site as a whole is free to enter, with admission charges for individual venues and attractions. Check festival dates when some venues may be otherwise closed.

Scan this QR code for more information and details of venues.

From Industry to Artistry

Exhibitions, gigs, films, festivals and other events at vast post-industrial space Westergas tap into Amsterdam's sustainability-driven creative spirit. This late-19th-century Dutch Renaissance complex designed by Isaac Gosschalk, previously known as Westergasfabriek, was the city's western coal-fired gasworks until production ceased in 1967. From the 1990s, the heavily polluted site was decontaminated and industrial architecture preserved, as artists and entrepreneurs realised its potential. In 2003, it evolved into an urban 'cultural village', and in 2018, new ownership reenergised its cultural output.

Museums & Galleries

Westergas' historic, renovated buildings are now home to a series of creative spaces, such as the grand former engineer's residence now hosting the artist-designed, 2025-opened **Museum Villa** *(museumvilla.com; adult/child from €17.50/9)*. Playful, experiential contemporary art is at the heart of its changing exhibitions.

The former purification hall, where sulphur was extracted, is home to the 2022-opened immersive digital art gallery **Fabrique des Lumières** *(fabrique-lumieres.com; adult/child €18/14)*. A hundred cutting-edge light projectors blast works by legendary artists such as Klimt and Hundertwasser across the industrial walls with immersive musical soundtracks. Alongside the main exhibitions are

WESTERGAS

digital explorations of themes like the creation of photons and underwater life.

Also in the purification hall is 2025 arrival **Amsterdam in Motion** *(amsterdaminmotion.nl; adult/child €18/free)*. Curated by the city's history museum, the Amsterdam Museum (undergoing renovations until 2028), it incorporates a 15-minute journey through Amsterdam's past via projection mapping on a 200-sq-metre city model of 30,500 buildings at 1:1300 scale, and upper-floor interactive installations showing the city's present and future.

Drinking & Dining

On-site brewery **Brouwerij Troost Westergas** *(brouwerijtroost.nl; brewery tours per person €10)* has big silver tanks cooking up saison, blond ale and smoked porter varieties, distils its own *jenever* (Dutch gin) and gin, and makes its sodas; brewery tours lasting 45 minutes take place on Saturdays.

There's also a slew of drinking and/or dining offerings as diverse as, among others, mussels and gin

TAKE A BREAK
Follow the aromas wafting from coffee roastery **Espressofabriek**. Westergas' branch of local bakery-cafe mini-chain De Bakkerswinkel (pictured above; p72) has a unique location in the old regulators house next to the drawbridge.

MUSIC FESTIVALS

Westergas is ground zero for a whole host of music festivals. They include July's open-minded electronic dance festival **Milkshake** *(milkshake festival.com)* and pre-festival **Mini Milkshake** *(forall wholove.com)*. This is the home base of the ADE Lab Village, growing the next generation of EDM artists and producers, as part of October's massive EDM industry conference/dance festival, the **Amsterdam Dance Event** *(ADE; amster dam-dance-event.nl)*.

(at **Mossel En Gin**), Algerian cuisine (at **Raïnaraï**), and Japanese street food and retro arcade games (at **TonTon Club**). You'll find plenty more throughout.

It's even possible to stay here at **Conscious Hotel Westerpark**, in the monumental 1885-built former gasworks office, powered by wind with recycled materials and aquaponic walls that grow the hotel cafe's vegetables and herbs.

Clubbing, Entertainment & Festivals

Entertainment options span a youth-oriented theatre, the **Theater De Krakeling** *(krakeling.nl)* to an arthouse cinema in the boiler house, **Het Ketelhuis** *(ketelhuis.nl)*, while clubbing spaces include **Radio Radio** *(radioradio.radio)*, with a DJ bar, club and radio station, and **WestWeelde** *(westweelde.nl)*, combining a huge nightclub, a bar/restaurant with a massive terrace and an events space – events sometimes spill over to the adjacent industrial shell of the old transformer house, **De Wester**. Westergas' most iconic cultural stage is the giant, cylindrical former gas storage tank, the **Gashouder** (undergoing renovations until late 2026), with concerts, events and festivals.

The roaming **Sunday Market** *(sundaymarket.nl)*, with art, fashion and design, sets up here on the first Sunday of each month from March to October. Westergas' calendar also includes May's food-truck feast **Rollende Keukens** *(rollendekeukens.amster dam)*, with over 100 'rolling kitchens'.

Westerpark

Linked to Westergas by a long wading pool and tree-shaded paths, expansive Westerpark has its roots in the city's earliest municipal park, originally established as the Westerplantsoen (Western Garden) in 1845 to provide workers with an escape from the industrial surrounds, and redeveloped after 1891 when the garden made way for the relocated western canal. Its lawns are a favourite hangout on sunny days.

Westerpark

Westerpark

Conscious
Hotel
Westerpark

Westergas

Museum
Villa

De Bakkerswinkel

Radio Radio

Het
Kelhuis

Amsterdam
in Motion

Theater De
Krakeling

Brouwerij
des
Troost

Westergas

WESTERPARK

Pazzanistr

Espressofabriek

Fabrique
des
Lumières

Haarlemmerweg

Groen van Prinstererstr

van de Hoopstr

Bestevaerstr

WestVeelde

De Wester

Gosschalklaan

Van Hallstr

Volkstuinenpark
Sloterdijkermeer

Gashouder

Mossel
En Gin

Potgieterkade

STAATSLIEDEN
-FREDERIK
HENDRIKBUURT

Ton Ton
Club

Rainarai

0.15 miles

300 m

☘ WALKING TOUR

Walk Western Canal Ring & Jordaan

Strolling the tiny streets and lanes of the Western Canal Ring and Jordaan gives you close-up views of historic structures, gabled canal houses and tiny former workers' dwellings, and opens a treasure chest of small, charming shops. These are Amsterdam's prime neighbourhoods for highly specialised boutiques selling items you'd find nowhere else – perfect for unhurried wandering.

START	END	LENGTH
Posthoornkerk	Winkel 43	4km; 2½hr

1 Hidden Church

Set back from shop-lined Haar-lemmerstraat, the neo-Gothic **Posthoornkerk** was built in 1863 by Pierre Cuypers, who went on to design the Rijksmuseum (p98) and Centraal Station. In the 1970s, residents saved the triple-spired church from demolition; it's now an events venue.

2 Herenmarkt Landmark

At the Herenmarkt's 17th-century **West-Indisch Huis**, the former Dutch West India Company (Geoctroyeerde Westindische Compagnie; GWC) HQ, its governors authorised the establishment of Nieuw Amsterdam (now New York City).

3 Literary Luminary

Dutch literary giant Eduard Douwes Dekker, pen name Multatuli, worked in colonial administration in Batavia (now Jakarta); his novel *Max Havelaar* (1860) made him a social conscience for the Netherlands. The **Multatuli Museum** has furniture and artefacts from his time in Indonesia, with a statue three blocks south on the Singel.

4 Ethical Boutique

In the tightly packed grid of the Negen Straatjes ('nine little streets'), **Marie-Stella-Maris** donates a percentage from its plant-based skincare products and home fragrances (including its signature sage, green tea and citrus scent, Objets d'Amsterdam) to support sustainable water initiatives around the world.

5 Dutch Design

Design platform **Frozen Fountain's** established and emerging artists, craftspeople and designers showcase striking furniture and interiors like rugs, light fittings, wall hooks, mirrors, candleholders, prints, photography and tapestries.

6 Historic Bruin Café

Stop for a frothy beer at wood-lined **Café Chris**, believed to be the Jordaan's oldest *bruin café*, dating from 1624, with workers building the Westertoren collecting their pay here. Its name comes from the owner who took over in 1957.

7 Distinctive Sweets

Corner shop **Het Oud-Hollandsch Snoepwinkeltje** is lined with jar after apothecary jar of Dutch penny sweets with flavours from chocolate to coffee and cardamom, all sorts of fruit, and the salty liquorice known as *zoute drop*. While *drop* (liquorice) is an acquired taste, some versions are stronger than others; ask for recommendations.

8 Apple Pie

Queuing for tasty, towering slices of still-warm, cinnamon-spiced *appeltaart* (apple pie) with some *slagroom* (whipped cream) at **Winkel 43** (p72) is a neighbourhood ritual on Mondays and Saturdays when market stalls fill the Noordermarkt (p68).

EXPERIENCES

Browse the Negen Straatjes

SHOPPING

In a city filled to the brim with shopping opportunities, the **Negen Straatjes** (MAP: ❶ P54 D7; *de9straatjes.nl*) represent an especially dense concentration.

Between Raadhuisstraat and Leidsegracht, each of these 'nine little streets' is just a block long. The streets (from west to east, and north to south: Reestraat, Hartenstraat, Gasthuismolensteeg, Berenstraat, Wolvenstraat, Oude Spiegelstraat, Runstraat, Huidenstraat, Wijde Heisteeg) and four canals (west to east: Prinsengracht, Keizergracht, Herengracht and Singel) form a tight grid packed with some 250 shops.

The shops are tiny too, and many are highly specialised. You'll find boutiques with everything from pure silk fabrics to buttons, beads, ceramic tiles, rare watches, vintage bags, vintage jewellery, leather goods, ceramics, art, antiques, candles, flowers and plants, board games, vinyl records and niche specialities, from flippers (and diving gear, at **Keesiedive**; MAP: ❷ P54 E7) to slippers (and slip-ons like clogs, at **Antonia**; MAP: ❸ P54 E6). Numerous fashion designers have flagship stores here.

Most shops open daily; plan to spend at least a couple of hours wandering here.

Marvel at the Making of the Canal Ring

MUSEUM

MAP: ❹ P54 E8

A 17th-century canal house on the Herengracht is a fitting place to discover the extraordinary engineering behind Amsterdam's canal ring. At the **Grachtenmuseum Amsterdam** (*grachten.museum; adult/child €17.50/9.50*), audio-guided tours in small groups of up to 12 people depart every 10 minutes to avoid overcrowding and take in its permanent exhibition. Its high-tech holograms, videos, cartoons, and scale models of the city and canal houses demonstrate how the canals and tilting houses lining them were constructed and the problem-solving that went in to the city's expansion. There are thought-provoking temporary exhibitions (such as Animals of the Canals). The history of the symmetrical Dutch Baroque house designed by Philips Vingboons is conveyed in glorious period rooms.

Visiting typically takes around 1½ to two hours in all. Weekend afternoons are busiest so try and come early midweek: the museum opens at noon on Mondays, 10am on other days. Last entry is at 4.30pm. Afterwards, you'll look at the surrounding canals in a whole different light.

Catch Contemporary Photographic Exhibitions MUSEUM

MAP: **5** P54 **E8**

A pair of 17th-century canal houses are the showcase for photography that captures the zeitgeist in its artistic expression and spirited enquiry at **Huis Marseille** (*huismarseille.nl; adult/child €12.50/free*). Its original building (Keizersgracht 401) was built around 1665 for French merchant Isaac Focquier (look for the map impression of Marseille's port on the facade's gable stone). Stuccowork and Jacob de Wit's ceiling painting were added the following century; the 18th-century garden house was reconstructed in 2003. Exhibition spaces and a depot fill the adjoining Keizersgracht 399.

In part to protect the light-sensitive photographs, there's no permanent display; instead, it mounts several major exhibitions each year, mainly curated from its own collection. Check the agenda to find out what's coming up: exhibitions typically last around three to four months, with the museum closed for a week between each one.

Hang Out in the Haarlemmerbuurt AREA

Between Centraal Station and Westerpark, the hive of activity in the **Haarlemmerbuurt** (*haarlemmerbuurtamsterdam.nl*) is a legacy of the Brouwersgracht's former shipyards, breweries and

BEST CANAL EXPLORATIONS

Pure Boats

MAP: **6** P54 **E5**

Boutique operator with beautiful small boats; options include 90-minute daytime 'highlights' trips (with apple pie) or evening trips (with cheese platters). *pureboats.com*

Miss G's Brunch Boat

MAP: **7** P54 **E5**

Combines 90-minute weekend cruises with brunches, beats and Bloody Marys. *missgs.nl*

Canal Motorboats

Amsterdam's first and oldest operator has rentals from **Westerdoksdijk** (MAP: **8** P54 **E1**), **Zandhoek** (MAP: **9** P54 **E1**) and **Westerpark** (MAP: **10** P54 **B2**), including 'plastic fishing' equipment to clean up the canals. *canalmotorboats.com*

Kayak in Amsterdam

MAP: **11** P54 **D8**

Guided one-hour 'Around Jordaan' tours pass landmarks like the Westerkerk. *kayakinamsterdam.com*

warehouses. The neighbourhood's spine stretches along Haarlemmerstraat past the **Posthoornkerk** (MAP: **12** P54 **E3**). Across the Prinsengracht, Haarlemmerstraat's western extension, the Haarlemmerdijk, continues to the neoclassical city gateway **Haarlemmerpoort** (MAP: **13** P54 **D2**) on the large square Haarlemmer-plein, home to a Wednesday *boerenmarkt* (farmers market).

Today, this 1km-long thoroughfare is a buzzing commercial strip, lined with independent boutiques stocking fashion (vintage and new), cosmetics, books, music and homewares, with an increasingly sustainable focus, as well as food and drink specialists. Also here is Amsterdam's oldest cinema, 1912 art-deco gem **The Movies** (MAP: ⓮ P54 D3; *themovies. nl*), showing indie and mainstream films (including films with English subtitles).

Treasure Hunt at the Jordaan's Markets   MARKET

With the 1623-built Calvinist church the **Noorderkerk** (MAP: ⓯ P54 E4; *noorderkerk.nl*), home to classical concerts *(noorder kerkconcerten.nl)* and with the immersive projections of **Van Gogh & Rembrandt in Amsterdam** *(vangoghinamsterdam.com; adult/child €17/13)* as its backdrop, the **Noordermarkt** (MAP: ⓰ P54 E4; *noordermarkt-amsterdam. nl*) has been a marketplace since the early 17th century.

Saturdays see the Noordermarkt host a general market in front of the church, with everything from antiques and bric-a-brac to artisan arts, crafts, ceramics, prints, posters, vintage fashion, bags, hats and jewellery, as well as a *boerenmarkt* with organic produce.

On Mondays, a general market takes over the Noordermarkt. Along the adjacent Westerstraat (once the Anjeliersgracht, meaning Carnation Canal, dug in 1650 and backfilled in 1861 to create a thoroughfare), the **Westerstraat Markt** (aka the Westermarkt) sells bolts of colourful fabrics.

Around the corner from the Noordermarkt, Saturday's lively **Lindengracht Markt** has been a neighbourhood tradition since 1894. Join locals browsing more than 230 stalls selling fresh fruit, vegetables, seafood, fabulous cheeses, breads and Dutch delicacies like caramel-filled *stroopwafels*, colourful cut flowers, clothing and homewares.

Learn about the National Flower   MUSEUM

MAP: ⓱ P54 D5

Allow around half an hour or so at the diminutive **Amsterdam Tulip Museum** *(amsterdamtulip museum.com; adult/child €7/4)*, which offers an overview of the history of the country's favourite bloom. Through exhibits, timelines and two short films (in English), you'll learn how Ottoman merchants encountered the flowers in the Himalayan steppes and began commercial production in Türkiye, how fortunes were made and lost during Dutch 'Tulipmania' in the 17th century, and how bulbs were used as food during WWII. You'll also discover present-day growing and harvesting techniques. There's a great collection of tulip art and artefacts such as vases designed to accommodate separate stems.

Even if you're not visiting the museum, you can stop by its gift shop overflowing with high-quality floral souvenirs (many artist commissions), including jewellery, bags, books, homewares like tea towels, aprons and tableware, and antique and reproduction Delft tiles. It also stocks a selection of premium bulbs in season (spring-flowering varieties in autumn and summer-flowering bulbs in spring/early summer).

Discover Boat Life in the Jordaan
MUSEUM

MAP: **18** P54 **D7**

Permanently moored on the Prinsengracht, the 23m-long *Hendrika Maria*, a former cargo ship from 1914, is now the **Houseboat Museum** *(houseboatmuseum. nl; adult/child €9.50/5)*. It offers a good sense of how *gezellig* (cosy, convivial) life can be on the water. Restored in 2008, there's some fantastic vintage decor from 1967 to 1997 when it was a residence. An audio guide lets you navigate its surprisingly spacious 80-sq-metre interior; the actual displays are minimal, but you can watch a presentation on houseboats (some pretty and some ghastly) and inspect the sleeping, living, cooking and dining quarters with all the mod cons.

Amsterdam's 2500-or-so houseboats are connected to utilities including water, electricity, gas and the sewage system, thanks to the city's Project Schoonschip (Project Clean Ship), which saw every houseboat connected to the sewage system by 2017, dramatically improving the water quality of the canals. Museum tickets are cheaper before noon (online bookings only).

 TULIPMANIA

The Dutch tulip craze of 1636–37 ranks alongside the greatest economic booms and busts in history. After success growing and cross-breeding tulips in the Netherlands' cool, damp climate, exotic frilly, flame-streaked specimens attracted the attention of wealthy merchants, and tulip growers arose to service the demand. A speculative frenzy ensued: many bulbs changed hands time and again before they sprouted. When traders failed to fetch expected prices in February 1637, the market collapsed. Within weeks many of the country's wealthiest merchants went bankrupt and many more people lost everything. Enthusiasm for tulips endured, however, and the Netherlands remains the world leader of tulip cultivation.

Stop by Johnny Jordaanplein

SQUARE

MAP: ⑲ P54 **D7**

Across the Prinsengracht from the houseboat museum (p69), **Johnny Jordaanplein** is a shady little square named after Johnny Jordaan (the pseudonym of Johannes Hendricus van Musscher), a popular musician in the mid-1900s who sang the romantic music known as *levenslied* (tears-in-your-beer-style ballads). On the square, you'll find Johnny, and members of the Jordaan musical hall of fame, cast in bronze. On national holiday King's Day, this is where many Jordaanians congregate for live music.

Meet Cats Aboard the Poezenboot

ANIMAL SANCTUARY

MAP: ⑳ P54 **F4**

Feline fans may want to check out a different kind of 'houseboat', the **Poezenboot** (*depoezenboot.nl; by donation*) a floating animal sanctuary on the Singel. It was

founded in 1966 by local woman Henriette van Weelde, who became legendary for looking after several hundred different stray cats at a time. The boat has since been taken over by a foundation and can hold some 50 kitties in proper pens. Some are permanent residents, and the rest are ready to be adopted (after being desexed and implanted with an identifying microchip, in line with Dutch law).

It's open from 1pm to 3pm on Tuesdays, Wednesdays and Saturdays; only six people are allowed onboard at a time and it doesn't take reservations, so arrive early and be prepared to wait in line if it's busy.

Have a Laugh

COMEDY

Catch comedy at several places in this neighbourhood. **Boom Chicago** (MAP: ㉑ P54 **C6**; *boomchicago.nl*) stages seriously funny improv-style comedy shows in English most nights, plus theme

🗎 GABLE STONES

Before street numbers were introduced in the 19th century, *gevelstenen* (gable stones) identified homes and businesses. Like stained-glass church windows, these stone tablets above doors on buildings' facades used illustrations (many with religious symbolism and imagery) as well as text. Some 850 exist today that tell stories of the people who lived and plied their trades here, like the horseshoe gable stone of the former blacksmith at Lindengracht 73; copper barrels used to make potash at the former soap maker at Tuinstraat 46; and goose-feather quill of the former scribe at Egelantiersstraat 52. Look up as you stroll.

nights and guest comedians, and runs two-hour improv taster classes on Saturdays.

Stand-up and open-mic nights in English and Dutch take place at the 1994-established **Comedy Café** (MAP: 22 P54 F2; *comedycafe.nl/ amsterdam*) on the IJ River.

Alternative living-room-like space **De Nieuwe Anita** (MAP: 23 P54 B6; *denieuweanita.nl*) has comedy along with emerging musicians, comedy, cult films, spoken word performances and more.

Travel Back a Century in Time

MUSEUM

MAP: 24 P54 D4

In the Jordaan, the **Pianola Museum** (*pianolamuseum. online; adult/child €9/5*) is a very special place, evoking the Art Nouveau to Art Deco eras of 1900 to 1935 and crammed with pianolas from the time. The museum has dozens, although fewer are on display at any given time, as well as more than 40,000 music rolls and a player pipe organ. It's open Friday, Saturday and Sunday afternoons for continuous tours, or by appointment. Intimate concerts are regularly held on the player pianos, featuring anything from Mozart to Fats Waller, as well as rare classical or jazz tunes

composed specially for the instrument – check dates and booking details on the website.

Delve into Digital Worlds

MUSEUM, ARCADE

In a massive 3000-sq-metre industrial warehouse west of Houthaven, **AMAZE** (MAP: 25 P54 A1; *amaze-amsterdam.com; adult/ child €26.95/15.50*) is a multi-sensory maze of light and sound installations, smoke, mirrors, lasers and beats that recall its former life as a nightclub. In small groups, you move through its different spaces (of varying intensity) in around an hour. From Centraal, take bus 22 (direction Sloterdijk) and alight at the Contactweg stop.

For a throwback to '90s digital nostalgia, the nearby **Blast Galaxy** (MAP: 26 P54 A1; *blastgalaxy.nl; adult/child €15/10, Mario Kart room per person €10, karaoke from €80*) has more than 100 retro arcade and console games like Donkey Kong, Double Dragon, Galaga, Mario Bros, Mortal Kombat, Pac-Man, Street Fighter, Tekken and Tetris. Admission includes unlimited games; you don't need additional coins or tokens. It's typically open Wednesday to Sunday.

Best Places for...

See p54 for map of locations

G Budget **GG** Midrange **GGG** Top End

Eating

Bakeries

Saint-Jean G
27 D4

Flaky croissants, danishes, cruffins, brioche and cinnamon buns, are among the 100% plant-based treats at this bright, white-painted corner bakery. *8am-5pm*

Louf G
28 B7

Turns out sourdough loaves, focaccia, Viennese pastries and has filled sandwiches; don't miss the *krentenbollen* (currant buns). *8am-3pm Mon-Sat, to noon Sun*

Petit Gâteau G
29 F4

Exquisite French pastries made on site: tartlets topped with jewel-like fruits, glazed éclairs, macarons, shell-shaped madeleine cakes and quiches. *10am-6pm*

Cafe Dining

De Bakkerswinkel G
30 C2

Uniquely situated at Westergas, with mezzanine seating, sofas and a sunny terrace, with great-value cafe dishes. *9am-5pm Mon-Fri, 10am-5pm Sat & Sun*

Eet Café Roem G
31 D5

Sandwiches, toasties and giant, thin sweet or savoury Dutch pancakes looking down the Leliegracht from the Prinsengracht. *9am-9pm Mon-Fri, 10am-9pm Sun*

Winkel 43 GG
32 E4

Popular from breakfast through to evening drinks, and for Amsterdam's most coveted *appeltaart*. *7am-1am Mon, 8am-1am Tue-Fri, 7am-2am Sat, 9am-1am Sun*

Refined Dining

De Belhamel GGG
33 F4

At the head of the Herengracht with canal-side tables, a split-level Art Nouveau interior and French-influenced breakfast through to dinner. *9.30am-10pm*

Wolf Atelier GGG
34 F3

Showcase for experimental chef Michael Wolf's four-, five- and 15-course tasting menus, with magical views at night. *6-10pm Tue-Fri, noon-5pm & 6-10pm Sat*

BAK GGG
35 E1

Overlooking the IJ River in a historic warehouse, crafting sustainable Dutch seafood, vegetables and wild game. *6-10pm Wed-Fri, 12.30-3pm & 6-10pm Sat & Sun*

Lars GGG
36 C1

Michelin-starred address at Houthaven using produce from its rooftop garden in three- to eight-course menus. *6-10pm Tue & Wed, noon-5pm & 6-10pm Thu-Sat*

Vegan

Koffie ende Koeck G
37 B2

Canal-side 'Coffee and Cookies' has an all-vegan menu spanning smoked tofu and pesto sandwiches, frittata, quiches and exceptional cakes. *10am-5pm Wed-Sun*

Madre
 D4

Skylit Mexican restaurant with dishes like artichoke tacos, sweet-potato quesadillas, or charred pineapple and mango tostadas. *5.30-10pm Mon-Fri, 11am-10.30pm Sat*

Men' Impossible
39 **D7**

Plant-based, zero-waste Japanese restaurant specialising in ramen with daily prepared handmade noodles as part of five-course menus, plus sake pairings. *5-10pm Wed-Mon*

Bonboon
40 **D6**

Elegant four- and five-course vegan menus served in bright Rozenstraat premises with herringbone timber floors, beautiful tiles and big picture windows. *6-11pm Wed-Sun*

Pizza

Lucca Due
41 **E3**

In the Posthoornkerk's old rectory, with red-checked tables on its tree-shaded summer terrace, and premium pizza toppings. *3-11pm Sun-Wed, to 11.30pm Thu-Sat*

Bella Storia
42 **E3**

Dough proved for 48 hours gives rise to pillowy bases topped with traditional ingredients and cooked in the wood-fired oven. *5.30-10pm Wed-Sun*

Yam Yam
43 **B5**

Contemporary trattoria turning out thin-crust pizzas: salami and fennel seed; smoked ham, mascarpone and truffle; and many vegetarian varieties. *5.30-10pm Wed-Sat*

Pazzi
44 **D7**

The original branch of the Amsterdam mini-chain where perfectly charred wood-fired pizzas are made with care and Italian beers are the ideal accompaniment. *5-10pm*

Drinking

Western Canal Ring Bruin Cafés

't Arendsnest
45 **E5**

Gorgeous *bruin café* with glowing copper *jenever* boilers, serving only Dutch beer, *jenevers*, ciders, whiskies and liqueurs.

noon-midnight Sun-Thu, to 1am Fri & Sat

Café Brandon
46 **E5**

Rare corner canal house dating back to 1626 adorned with B&W pictures of the Dutch royals and Ajax players. *3pm-1am Mon-Thu, noon-3am Fri & Sat, noon-1am Sun*

Café het Molenpad
47 **D8**

Quietly romantic, with low lamps and candlelight illuminating its small tables beneath pressed-tin ceilings. *noon-1am Sun-Thu, to 2am Fri & Sat*

Proeflokaal A van Wees
48 **E7**

Pours its Jordaan-distilled house brands – 17+ *jenevers* and 60+ liqueurs. *11am-11pm Sun-Thu, to 1am Fri & Sat*

Jordaan Bruin Cafés

't Smalle
49 **D5**

Dock your boat at this 1786 former *jenever* distillery with its convivial terrace. *2pm-midnight Mon-Thu, to 1am Fri & Sat, to 10pm Sun*

Café Papeneiland
50 **E4**

With Delft Blue tiles and a central stove, this *bruin café* is a 1642 gem. *10am-1am Mon-Thu,*

10am-3pm Fri & Sat, noon-1am Sun

Café Pieper
 51 D8

Antique beer mugs hang from the bar with a 1875 working Belgian beer pump at this stained-glass-windowed 1665 treasure. *noon-1am Sun-Thu, to 2am Fri & Sat*

De Twee Zwaantjes
52 D5

Opened in 1921, the 'Two Swans' is at its liveliest during Wednesday-night *levenslied* (ballad) sing-alongs. *noon-1am Wed, Thu & Sun, to 3am Fri & Sat*

Cocktail Bars

Vesper
53 E3

Memorabilia-filled James Bond–inspired bar with twists like blue-corn foam, green-olive spherification and gold-dust-infused vodka. *6pm-1am Wed-Sat*

Bar Oldenhof
54 D7

Speakeasy evoking the roaring 1920s with dimly lit dark-wood panelling, velvet armchairs and a jazz soundtrack. *6pm-1am Sun-Thu, to 2am Fri & Sat*

Sins of Sal
55 D4

Dark, vampire-themed Latin cocktail den mixing mezcal and tequila with cactus leaf and fermented

guava. *6pm-midnight Tue-Thu, to 2am Fri & Sat*

Rum Barrel
56 C1

Caribbean-style bar with over 300 different rums, fresh tropical juices and homemade infusions. *6pm-midnight Wed & Thu, to 2.30am Fri & Sat*

Coffee

Caffè il Momento
 57 E5

Exposed-brick space with a wall stencil of Amsterdam's canal houses, quality espresso and great coffee art. *8am-6pm Mon-Fri, 9am-5pm Sat & Sun*

Luuk's
58 E4

Espresso brews with pea protein, oat, coconut or dairy, plus matcha and the Jordaan's best banana bread. *7.30am-4.30pm Mon-Fri, 8am-5pm Sat, 9am-5pm Sun*

Rum Baba
59 C7

On Elandsgracht, selling its own-roasted beans, and brewing them to drink in or take with you to go. *8am-4.30pm Mon-Fri, 9am-5pm Sat & Sun*

Shopping

Fashion

BrandMission
60 F4

High-end men's and women's sustainable fashion along with handmade jewellery and vegan footwear. *noon-6pm Mon, 10am-6pm Tue-Sat, 1-5pm Sun*

Rain Couture
61 D7

Multi-seasonal wet-weather trench coats, jackets and parkas for men and women, plus hats and gloves, all made with sustainable fabrics. *11am-6pm Tue-Sat, noon-6pm Sun & Mon*

De Mof
62 E3

Durable work- and casual-wear since 1885; historical collections inspire its Waddenzee fishers' jumpers and coal workers' black jackets. *1-6pm Mon, 10am-6pm Tue-Fri, 10am-5pm Sat*

Vintage

Zipper
63 E8

Vintage clothing from the 1950s to '90s: fleece-lined suede jackets, patterned shirts, sunglasses, shoes...

11am-6pm Tue-Sat, noon-6pm Sun & Mon

Laura Dols
 64 E7

Everything from 1920s beaded dresses to '40s hand-stitched leather gloves, bags, shawls and jewellery, and vintage wedding dresses. *11am-6pm Mon-Wed & Sat, 11am-7pm Thu & Fri, noon-6pm Sun*

2nd Culture
65 E3

Awesome for second-hand streetwear, rare sneakers, sportswear, art and accessories. *11.30am-6.30pm*

Design & Homewares

POLSPOTTEN
66 D5

Brand store of the 1986-founded Dutch design pioneer, with colourful furniture, textiles, tableware (teapots, jugs) and quirky decorative pieces. *10am-6pm Tue-Sat*

StoryTiles
67 E7

Hand-fired ceramic tiles: house numbers, Amsterdam streetscapes, windmills, bicycles, canals, constellations and botanicals. *10am-6pm*

DSIGN
 68 E7

Locally themed items include Piet Design paper

houses and glass tulips, Nijntje (Miffy) LED lamps, CRE8 canal wall hangers and more. *10am-7pm*

Antiques & Secondhand

Antiekcentrum Amsterdam
 69 C7

Cornucopia art, antiques, vintage and collectibles spread over 1750 sq metres. *11am-6pm Mon & Wed-Fri, to 5pm Sat & Sun*

Distortion Records
70 D4

Vinyl from the 1970s onwards in genres ranging from punk and funk to alternative, indie, garage, grunge, industrial, electro, hip-hop, acid jazz and neo-folk. *11am-6pm Tue, Wed & Fri, 11am-9pm Thu, 10am-6pm Sat*

Gourmet Treats

De Kaaskamer
71 D7

Stacked with over 400 different, mostly Dutch cheeses. Vacuum-packing available. *8am-8pm Mon, Thu & Fri, 8am-6.30pm Tue & Wed, 8am-6pm Sat, 9am-7pm Sun*

Jordino
72 E3

Chocolate creations include chocolate tulips and famous Dutch paintings (great choc-dipped

ice cream, too). *1-6pm Mon, 10am-6pm Tue-Sat*

Arnold Cornelis
 73 D7

Long-standing shop with cakes (eg fruitcake, cheesecake), biscuits, chocolates (including liqueur-filled varieties) and candies. *8.30am-6pm Mon-Fri, to 5pm Sat*

Buufs Keuken
74 E5

All-local infused vinegars, chutneys, sauces, confectionery, chocolates, beer, wine, cider and soft drinks; also does mini picnic boxes. *10am-4pm Mon-Thu, 9am-4pm Fri & Sat*

Drinks Galore

World of Nix
75 D4

Non-alcoholic beers, wines and spirits, mocktails, cordials, mixers, teas, kombucha and infused sparkling waters. *11am-6pm Mon-Wed, 11am-7pm Thu, 10am-7pm Fri & Sat, noon-5pm Sun*

De Ware Jacob
76 E5

Independent bottle shop with Dutch and European wines, local *jenevers*, beers and ciders. *10.30am-7pm Mon-Fri, 9.30am-6pm Sat, noon-6pm Sun*

🚶 **WALKING TOUR**

Wander the Western Islands & Houthaven

Amsterdam's past, present and future sustainability is on show on this walk (or ride – you can cycle this route). It leads through the city's peaceful Western Islands, with historic links to the city's maritime heritage, to the innovative architecture of one of the city's newest neighbourhoods, the former lumber ports of Houthaven.

START	END	LENGTH
Great Bubble Barrier (bus 48 Westerdoksdijk)	REM (bus 48 Haparandaweg)	4.75km; 3hr

① Ingenious Bubbles

At Westerdok, look for a diagonal line of bubbles. A pioneering green initiative, this 2019-installed **Great Bubble Barrier** lifts plastic waste to the surface where it flows to a collection point without hindering the passage of fish or watercraft.

② Repurposed Silos

Located on a former breakwater, and incorporating 1896 grain silos and a modern 2003 extension designed like stacked shipping containers, **Silodam**, a 10-storey building of apartments and commercial spaces, has a huge wooden-decked viewing platform on its eastern side overlooking the IJ River.

③ Historic Harbour

The **Zandhoek** is a photogenic stretch of Western Islands waterfront on Realeneiland's eastern shore. It's now a modern yacht harbour, but back in the 17th century it was a 'sand market', where ships would purchase bagfuls for ballast. Many ships' captains lived in the area.

④ Three Herrings Bridge

Linking the Western Islands of Realeneiland and Prinseneiland, the double wooden drawbridge **Drieharingenbrug** ('Three Herrings Bridge') is named for the gable stone on the 18th-century house on its northern side.

⑤ Maritime Mural

Covering four building facades on Van Diemenstraat's southern side is **Muurschildering Willem Barentsz**, a series of Delft-Blue murals (2008) by Klaartje Bruyn depicting the explorations of Dutch seafarer and scientist Willem Barentsz, who in the late 1500s attempted three expeditions to find a northeast passage through the Arctic to Asia and the Far East (all were unsuccessful due to ice).

⑥ Riverside Dip

Industrial 1876-dug harbour Houthaven (aka Houthavens; 'lumber ports') has been transformed since 2010, with seven artificial islands now comprising Amsterdam's first climate-neutral neighbourhood. Cool off at public-access IJ swimming platform **Het Eikenhout**, with stunning views of the gateway-like Pontsteiger building.

⑦ Pirate Broadcasting Rig Turned Restaurant

Rising 22m from the IJ River, red-metal rig **REM** was a pirate radio and TV broadcasting station in the North Sea off the coast of Noordwijk in 1964 until being shut down. In 2011, the rig was towed here and now houses a one-of-a-kind restaurant with 360-degree views from its three platforms, including the former helipad rooftop terrace.

See p91
for eating,
drinking and
shopping
listings

Explore
Southern Canal Ring

Researched by
Barbara Woolsey &
Catherine Le Nevez

A horseshoe-shaped loop of parallel canals immediately south of the centre, the Southern Canal Ring is a sight in itself: together with the Western Canal Ring, its canals form the UNESCO World Heritage–listed Grachtengordel. The Southern Canal Ring has long been one of Amsterdam's main entertainment districts, home to wonderfully atmospheric theatres and cinemas, legendary music venues, a thriving LGBTIQ+ scene and the tourist-magnet nightlife hubs of Leidseplein and Rembrandtplein. Between the two squares, the grand waterways are lined by some of the city's most elegant canal houses, a cache of museums, a flower market, and waterside restaurants and bars.

Getting Around

 Walking

Walking is the perfect way to take in this neighbourhood's magnificent architecture and interesting boutiques.

 Tram

This area is well served by trams. For the Leidseplein area, take tram 1, 2, 5, 7, 12, 17 or 19. To reach Rembrandtplein, take tram 4, which travels down Utrechtsestraat, or tram 14. Tram 24 runs along the neighbourhood's southeastern edge, turning south to De Pijp.

 Metro

Line 52 between Amsterdam Noord and Zuid stops at Vijzelgracht.

Café Americain (p85)
WOLF·PHOTOGRAPHY/SHUTTERSTOCK

THE BEST

CANAL-HOUSE RESIDENCE
Museum Van Loon (p82)

ART EXHIBITIONS
H'ART (p86)

PHOTO OP
Reguliersgracht ('Canal of Seven Bridges'; p86)

CONTEMPORARY PHOTOGRAPHY
Foam (p87)

MUSIC VENUE
Melkweg (p88)

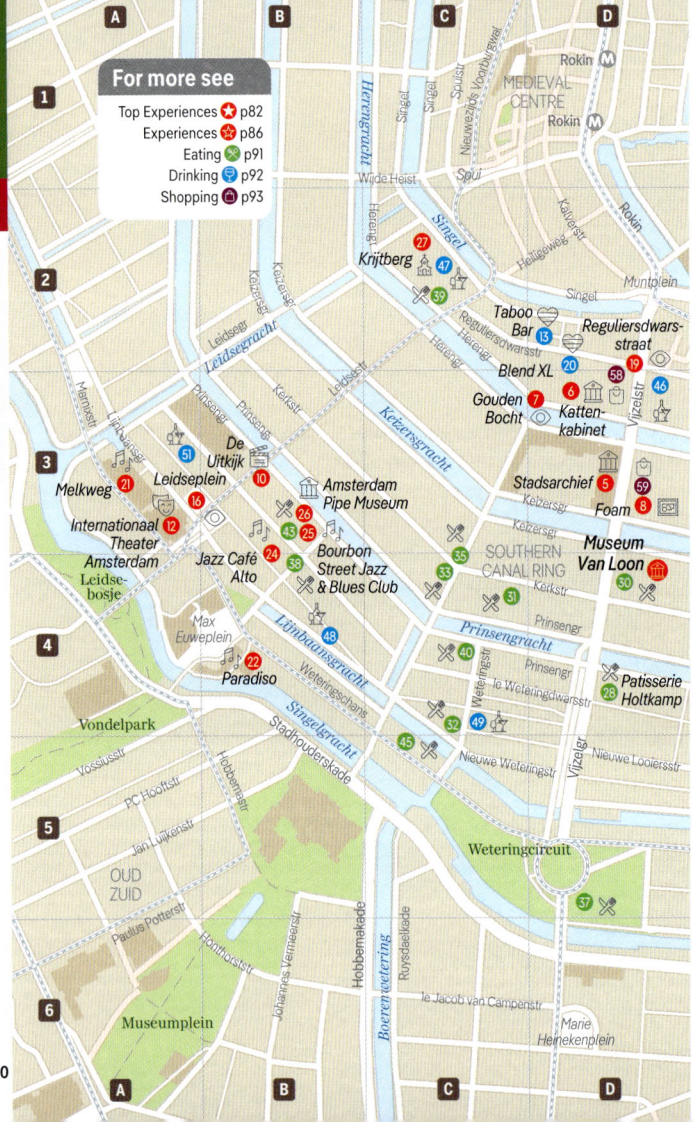

For more see

Top Experiences ⭐ p82
Experiences ✴ p86
Eating 🟢 p91
Drinking 🔵 p92
Shopping 🟣 p93

MEDIEVAL
CENTRE

Rokin Ⓜ

Rokin Ⓜ

Spui

Wijde Heist

Singel

Krijtberg 27
47
39

Taboo
Bar 13

Reguliersdwarsstraat 20

Blend XL

Gouden 7
Bocht 6

Katten-
kabinet

Reguliersdwars-
straat

58
19
46

Stadsarchief 5

Foam 8
59

Museum
Van Loon

50

SOUTHERN
CANAL RING

De Uitkijk 10
51

Melkweg 21

Leidseplein

16

Internationaal
Theater
Amsterdam 12

Amsterdam
Pipe Museum

26
43 25
35

Bourbon
Street Jazz
& Blues Club

55

31

Jazz Café
Alto 24

Leidse-
bosje

Lijnbaansgracht 48

Max
Euweplein

40

Paradiso 22

Patisserie
Holtkamp 28

32
49

Vondelpark

45

Nieuwe Wetering str

OUD
ZUID

Weteringcircuit

57

Museumplein

Marie
Heinekenplein

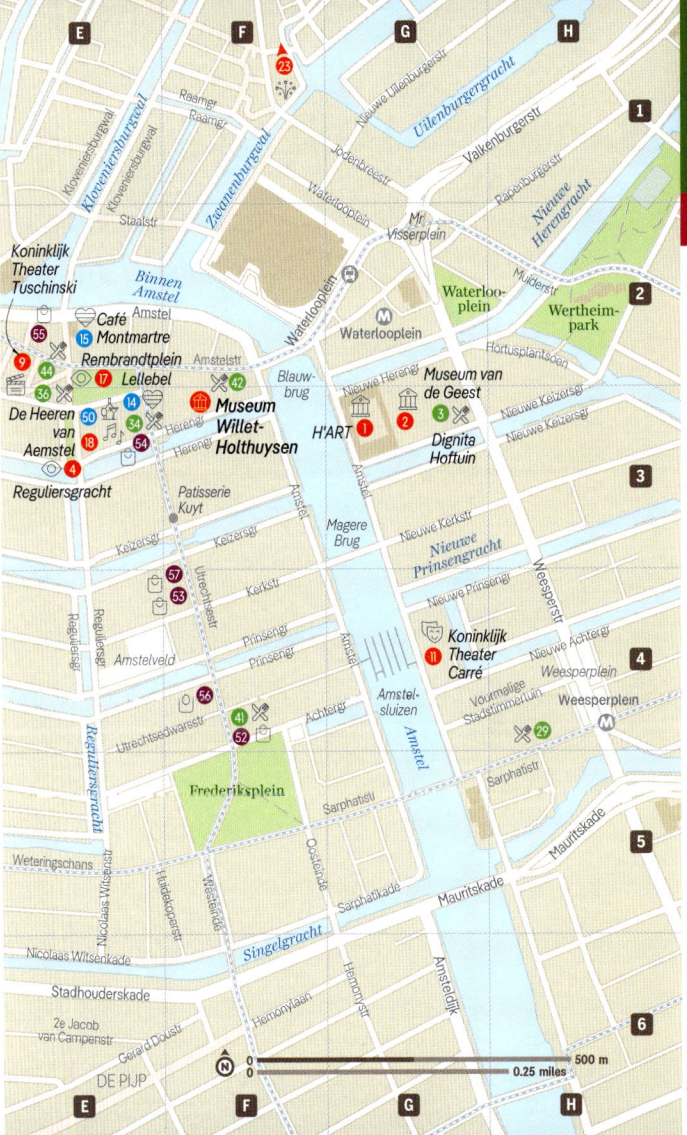

Koninklijk
Theater
Tuschinski

Binnen
Amstel

Café
Montmartre

Amstel

Rembrandtplein

Lellebel

De Heeren
van
Aemstel

Reguliersgracht

Museum
Willet-
Holthuysen

Blauw-
brug

Nieuwe Herengr

H'ART

Museum van
de Geest

Dignita
Hoftuin

Waterlooplein

Waterlooplein

Wertheim-
park

Mr
Visserplein

Jodenbreestr

Waterloopstr

Uilenburgergracht

Nieuwe
Herengracht

Valkenburgerstr

Rapenburgerstr

Staalstr

Zwanenburgwal

Klovenniersburgwal

Raamgr

Raamgr

Patisserie
Kuyt

Magere
Brug

Nieuwe Kerkstr

Nieuwe
Prinsengracht

Nieuwe Prinsengr

Koninklijk
Theater
Carré

Amstel-
sluizen

Weesperplein

Voormalige
Stadstimmertuin

Weesperplein

Sarphatistr

Frederiksplein

Sarphatistr

Sarphatikade

Mauritskade

Mauritskade

Weteringschans

Singelgracht

Nicolaas Witsenkade

Stadhouderskade

2e Jacob
van Campenstr

DE PIJP

Amsteldijk

Hemonylaan

Hemonystr

0   500 m

0.25 miles

N

⭐ **TOP EXPERIENCE**

Museum Van Loon

Built in 1672, this beautiful canal house–museum was first home to acclaimed painter Ferdinand Bol. By the late 1800s, the Van Loons, a prominent patrician family, had moved in and have lived here ever since; they still occupy the building's upper floors.

MAP P80 **D4**

PLANNING TIP
The hop-on, hop-off **Cultuur Ferry** (*cultuurferry.nl*) stops at Museum Van Loon, see the website for times. Tickets to the museum are separate (book ahead online).

Scan this QR code for full opening hours and to book tickets.

Art & Interiors

The house is filled with opulent furniture and family portraits that seem to whisper secrets as you pass from room to gorgeous room. Among the 150 portraits of the Van Loon family, you'll see important paintings such as The Marriage of Willem van Loon and Margaretha Bas by Jan Miense Molenaer. But the main exhibit is the house itself. It's full of set-piece interior decoration, with intricate wedding-cake stucco on the ceilings, a garden room overlooking the formal hedges of the garden, and the glorious – but surely nightmare-inducing – decoration of the guest bedroom.

Temporary art exhibitions and concerts take place throughout the rooms.

Basement, Courtyard & Coach House

Downstairs you'll find the old-fashioned basement kitchen, where cook Leida presided for almost 40 years. Original blueprints were used to restore the 2017-opened wine cellar, pantry and storage room.

Outside, this is the only such mansion where you can still see a rear coach house, which once housed up to eight horse-drawn carriages at the end of the pristine formal courtyard garden. The small cafe in the coach house is a lovely place for a coffee and *appelschnitt* (apple strudel with currants, raisons, almonds and cinnamon) from **Patisserie Kuyt**.

⭐ **TOP EXPERIENCE**

Museum Willet-Holthuysen

Built in 1687 for Amsterdam mayor Jacob Hop and redesigned in 1739, this house-museum offers insight into the 19th-century lives of the merchant class' super-rich. It's named for Louisa Willet-Holthuysen, who lived a lavish, bohemian life here with her husband Abraham from 1861.

MAP P80 **F3**

Interiors & Exhibitions

Louisa Willet-Holthuysen left the property to the city in 1895; it's now managed by the city's history museum, the under-renovation Amsterdam Museum.

Strolling through the patrician house, you'll find plenty of information illustrating the lifestyle and interests of Abraham and Louisa. They were keen art collectors, and the rich selection of furniture and art includes notable paintings by Jacob de Wit. Also look for the place de milieu (centrepiece) that was part of the family's 275-piece Meissen table service in the Louis XVI–style ground-floor dining room, and the original 17th-century stained-glass windows upstairs. Downstairs, the preserved kitchen and scullery provide a glimpse of the work required to keep the house running, with simple decoration and lovely original tiling on the walls.

Every six months, a leading artist or collector is offered the opportunity to exhibit throughout the property's fabulous rooms.

The Garden

The intimate garden with a sundial is a reconstruction dating from 1972, created in the French classical style as was fashionable in the 19th century. It was originally smaller, as a coach house occupied some of the space. You can also peek at the garden through the iron fence at the Amstelstraat end.

PLANNING TIP
Mornings and weekends, when big museums are busy, are the quietest times to visit this museum. Its garden is a highlight of June's **Open Tuinen Dagen** (Open Garden Days; *opentuinen dagen.nl*).

Scan this QR code for full opening hours and to book tickets.

WALKING TOUR

Stroll the Southern Canal Ring

Amsterdam's lavish 17th-century lifestyle is on full show in the Southern Canal Ring. Most of the area was built at the end of the century, when Amsterdam was wallowing in wealth from the era's seafaring trade. A wander through reveals grand mansions, swanky antique shops, historic and futuristic tributes to Rembrandt, and a stately theatre.

START	END	LENGTH
Bloemenmarkt	Café Americain	2.2km; 1½hr

❶ Flower Market

Since 1860, Amsterdam's canal-side **Bloemenmarkt** (Flower Market) has been located here at the spot where growers would sail up the Amstel and moor their barges to sell their wares directly to customers. Now perched on piles, exotic bulbs are the main stock today (along with kitschy souvenirs).

❷ Amsterdam's Oldest Surviving Statue

Rembrandtplein was first called Reguliersplein, then Botermarkt for the butter markets held here until the mid-19th century. It gained its current name in 1876, when Louis Royer's 1852 iron statue of the painter, the **Rembrandt Monument**, which was cast in a single piece, was moved from the edge of the square to take pride of place in the centre.

❸ Merchant Mansions

During the 17th century, the Herengracht's **Gouden Bocht** (Golden Bend) was where the wealthiest Amsterdammers built when city expansion created deeper plots for rear gardens with unprecedented building permissions: gables were allowed to be twice as wide as the standard Amsterdam model.

❹ Spiegelkwartier Antiques

The perfect Delft vase or 16th-century wall map will most assuredly be hiding among the antique stores, bric-a-brac shops and commercial art galleries in the **Spiegelkwartier**. In the early 20th century, dealers set up shop around Spiegelstraat, with surrounding stately canal houses ensuring a steady flow of collectors. Hoogkamp Antiquariaat (Prints & Maps Hoogkamp) has wonderful prints of Amsterdam.

❺ Rembrandt Recreation

Steps from Leidesplein, digital museum **Rembrandts Amsterdam Experience** is a 25-minute immersion into Rembrandt's 17th-century time, brought startlingly to life by 5D special effects and interactive highlights like creating AI portraits in Rembrandt's style.

❻ Landmark Theatre

The neo-Renaissance **Internationaal Theater Amsterdam** was built in 1894; when it opened, public criticism of architect Jan Springer's design was so fierce that the exterior decorations were never completed.

❼ Grand Cafe

Nicknamed 'Amsterdam's living room', 1902-opened, Art Nouveau **Café Americain**, with potted palms, whirring fans and dizzyingly high ceilings, has huge stained-glass windows overlooking Leidseplein and a great terrace.

EXPERIENCES

View Art with H'ART
MUSEUM

This monumental 1683 building with its 102m-long facade on the Amstel was a satellite of St Petersburg's State Hermitage Museum. In the wake of the Russo-Ukranian War, the museum formally severed ties and rebranded as **H'ART** (MAP: ① P80 **G3**; *hartmuseum.nl; adult/ child €38.50/free*). Now with an emphasis on contemporary art, the new, independent museum offers three or four exhibitions per year and programming from diverse perspectives and cultures. The Smithsonian American Art Museum, British Museum and Centre Pompidou are among an impressive roster of archive and upcoming collabs.

In a separate wing, the **Museum van de Geest** (Museum of the Mind; MAP: ② P80 **G3**) has single, changing exhibitions spotlighting 'outsider art' produced by artists while in psychiatric institutions.

H'ART's front courtyard is home to the museum's **Grand Café** in summer (on the indoors upper level in winter).

In the leafy garden is the glass-walled cafe **Dignita Hoftuin** (MAP: ③ P80 **G3**).

Stroll around the park to see some beautiful monuments including the Daniel Libeskind–designed national Holocaust monument.

Photograph the Seven Bridges
BRIDGES

MAP: ④ P80 **E3**

One of Amsterdam's most romantic canals flows through this neighbourhood. The **Reguliersgracht**, aka the 'canal of seven bridges', is especially enchanting by night, when its humpbacked arches glow with tiny gold lights, creating rings that reflect on the water.

Though the best views are from aboard a boat, you can still get great vistas from land. Stand with your back to the Thorbeckeplein and with the Herengracht flowing directly in front of you to the left and right. Lean over the bridge and look straight ahead down the Reguliersgracht. It's one of the most photographed canal views in Amsterdam, sometimes nicknamed the 'necklace of bridges'.

Explore the Municipal Archives
ARCHIVES

MAP: ⑤ P80 **D3**

A distinctive striped former bank dating from 1923 now houses over 50km of shelving at the **Stadsarchief** (Amsterdam City Archives; *amsterdam.nl/ stadsarchief*). Amsterdam archival gems, such as the 1942 police report on the theft of Anne Frank's bike and a letter from Charles Darwin to Artis Zoo in 1868, can be viewed in the enormous tiled basement vault. Upstairs, a gallery space mounts temporary exhibits.

Admire Feline Art on the Golden Bend
MUSEUM

Wealthy financier Bob Meijer founded an entire museum in memory of his late red tomcat John Pierpont Morgan III. The **Kattenkabinet** (Cat Cabinet; MAP: ⑥ P80 **D3**; *adult/child €12.50/ 7.50*) collection includes artworks by Tsuguharu Foujita, Théophile Alexandre Steinlen and Amsterdam's chief sculptor, Hildo Krop. You may even get the chance to admire the cats that live in the building alongside the curious art collection.

A visit here gives you the opportunity to explore one of the famously double-wide, anything-but-humble canal-side homes on the **Gouden Bocht** (Golden Bend; MAP: ⑦ P80 **D3**); this is the only one open to the public.

Take in Photography at Foam
MUSEUM

MAP: ⑧ P80 **D3**

A visit to **Foam** (*foam.org; adult/ child €16/11.75*) is always an eye-opening experience. One of the world's leading museums for international photographic exhibitions, the diverse programming spans fashion retrospectives to travel photography. From the outside, Foam (short for 'Fotografiemuseum') looks like a grand canal house, but these three buildings, which are linked by staircases and passageways, are

BEST CINEMAS & THEATRES
Koninklijk Theater Tuschinski
MAP: ⑨ P80 **E2**
First completed in 1921 and has a capacity of 1431. This cinema is worth visiting alone for its sumptuous Art Deco interior alone. Has a Wurlitzer organ. *pathe.nl*

De Uitkijk
MAP: ⑩ P80 **B3**
This arthouse cinema in a 17th-century warehouse on the Prinsengracht, offers a mix of genres and countries, as well as classics and more recent films. *uitkijk.nl*

Koninklijk Theater Carré
MAP: ⑪ P80 **G4**
Historic Amstel theatre with circus, queer cabaret, musicals and comedy. *carre.nl*

Internationaal Theater Amsterdam
MAP: ⑫ P80 **A3** Has a 1200-capacity auditorium for large-scale plays, operettas and festivals. *ita.nl* (Hosts late May/early June's Holland Festival, the Netherlands' biggest arts festival, *hollandfestival.nl*).

the backdrop for spacious galleries, with an emphasis on showing experimental installations.

The **Foam Editions** gallery, featuring established and emerging photographers, supports the museum's educational projects.

TOP LGBTIQ+ PICKS

Taboo Bar
MAP: **13** P80 **D2**

Gay favourite Taboo has plentiful cocktail specials, drag shows and party games like bingo. *taboobar.nl*

Lellebel
MAP: **14** P80 **E3**

Alternative indie grunge rock queer bar with themed nights including karaoke, drag shows and comedy. *lellebel.nl*

Montmartre
MAP: **15** P80 **E2**

Crammed gay bar that's long been locally loved (it opened in 1982). Known for its Dutch ballads, karaoke, drag, and '80s and '90s hits. *cafemontmartre.nl*

Some of Foam's rotating exhibitions require an additional charge.

Hit the Nightlife Zones   NIGHTLIFE

Historic architecture, bars, pubs, clubs, theatres and live-music venues – **Leidseplein** (MAP: **16** P80 **A3**) has a bit of everything. The square and its surrounding streets are always busy, especially since several tram lines converge here. After dark, Leidseplein is a major nightlife hub that gets thronged by a mainstream crowd of party lovers (more tourists than locals). Pavement cafes at the northern end are perfect for people-watching. Wander along Lijnbaansgracht and Korte Leidsedwarsstraat where you'll find diverse options for dinner and drinks.

If you're looking for more action, nearby nightlife hub **Rembrandtplein** (MAP: **17** P80 **E2**)is ringed by cafes, pubs and clubs; popular places include **De Heeren van Aemstel** (MAP: **18** P80 **E3**) and Café Schiller (p92).

Party on Reguliersdwarsstraat   LGBTIQ+

The Southern Canal Ring has a longstanding, lively queer scene. Romp through some of its best nightlife on its major gay street, **Reguliersdwarsstraat** (MAP: **19** P80 **D2**). The pedestrian strip is lined by gay bars and nightclubs, cocktail joints and restaurants enjoyed by a diverse (gender, age and otherwise) crowd. Warm, summer evenings see everyone – partygoers to drag queens – melt outside into one big street party.

Gay nightlife institutions here include the twinkling disco-ball-lit dance floor at **Blend XL** (MAP: **20** P80 **D2**).

Dance at Legendary Venues   LIVE MUSIC, CLUBBING

In a former dairy factory squatted and repurposed by a theatre collective in 1970, the nonprofit **Melkweg** (Milky Way; MAP: **21** P80 **A3**; *melkweg.nl*) is one of the

Netherlands' most important concert venues, hosting up to 1500 people for DJs, club nights and live bands – everything from reggae to punk, heavy metal and mellow singer-songwriters. Its free, weekly 'Techno Tuesday' is a decade-long institution seeing hundreds of people stomp to high-BPM beats. Check for cutting-edge cinema, theatre and multimedia offerings, too.

In 1968, a beautiful 19th-century church was turned into the 'Cosmic Relaxation Center Paradiso'. Today, at the **Paradiso** (MAP: **22** P80 **B4**; *paradiso.nl*), a smaller hall hosts emerging artists, but there's something special about the main hall, where it seems the stained-glass windows might shatter under the force of synthesiser beats.

Both venues are associated with unforgettable ADE nights – tickets to events sell out quickly.

Take in Live Jazz Around the Ring
JAZZ

The neighbourhood's postwar exodus of wealthy residents, moving to bigger, greener suburbs, was a boon for inner city Amsterdam's underground culture. Small, canal-side buildings and basements were transformed into intimate spaces for live-music venues and cultural spaces; most notably, jazz clubs.

The historic **Jazz Café Alto** (MAP: **24** P80 **B3**; *jazz-cafe-alto. nl; admission Sun-Thu/Fri-Sat €5/€10*) has been staging jams and performances in the area since 1953. This is an atmospheric *bruin café*–style venue for serious jazz and (occasionally) blues. Find live gigs nightly – it doesn't take reservations so arrive as close to opening as possible if you want to snag a seat. Admission to live shows is still modest; jam sessions are free.

Meanwhile, **Bourbon Street Jazz & Blues Club** (MAP: **25** P80 **B3**; *bourbonstreet.nl*) is a modern

 AMSTERDAM DANCE EVENT

Thanks to its historic, large-scale theatres and nightlife, the Southern Canal Ring plays a big role in the **Amsterdam Dance Event** (ADE; MAP: **23** P80 **F1**), one of Europe's biggest electronic-music festivals. For five days every late October, over 500,000 participants – DJs, labels and clubbers, and everyone in between – come to dance to their favourite DJs and genres in massive club nights. During the day, though, ADE gets a little serious with a conference-like atmosphere and talks on sound production, trends and getting along in the industry.

venue keeping the neighbour-hood's live-music tradition alive. This intimate venue has a full and eclectic music programme. Check the website for a list of open jam sessions and performances ranging from jazz, blues and soul to rock, Latin and pop.

Marvel at Smoking Antiques
MUSEUM

MAP: 26 P80 B3

In a grand 17th-century canal house, the unexpectedly fascinating **Amsterdam Pipe Museum** (*pipemuseum.nl; adult/child €15/7.50*) spans more than 25,000 pipes dating across two millennia and several continents (only about 2000 items are displayed at once).

Guided tours (book your ticket ahead with a time slot) show the earliest South American pipes, 15th-century Dutch pipes, Chinese opium pipes, African ceremonial pipes and much more. At the heart of the collection is Dutch collector Don Duco who gathered the collection from around 60 countries over 40 years.

Attend Latin Mass at De Krijtberg
CHURCH

MAP: 27 P80 C2

The spiky spires of the Catholic church **Krijtberg** (*krijtberg.nl; free*) are an unmissable landmark amid rows of handsome Singel homes. Officially known as the St Franciscus Xaveriuskerk,

Krijtberg (Chalk Hill) replaced a clandestine Jesuit chapel on the same site in 1883; it's remained Jesuit to this day. If you get the chance, have a peek inside the neo-Gothic church; the interior is typically, lavishly Jesuit, covered with paintings and statuary. English mass is held on Saturdays at 5.15pm, and on some religious holidays. On Sundays at 10.30am, the Latin Mass followed by Gregorian chanting at 12.30pm can be a moving spiritual experience.

Savour Royal Dutch Treats
PATISSERIE

MAP: 28 P80 D4

Head to **Patisserie Holtkamp** (*patisserieholtkamp.nl*) to savour authentic Dutch treats fit for royalty. Check out the gilded royal coat of arms, topped by a crown, on the building's facade before entering; the historic patisserie is where the Dutch royals stock up. Founded in 1886, the gorgeous Art Deco interior (added in 1928 by architect Piet Kramer) is a feast for the eyes.

Delicacies include creamy cakes, meringue-topped tarts and Dutch pastries such as *amandelkrullen* (almond curls). Holtkamp is most famous for *kroketten* (croquettes), with fillings ranging from veal to prawns, which are on the menus of some of the city's top restaurants.

Best Places for...

ⓖ Budget　ⓖⓖ Midrange　ⓖⓖⓖ Top End

See p80 for map of locations

Eating

Bakeries

Bakhuys Amsterdam ⓖ
 29 H4

In a large industrial space, watch from up close as bakers knead sourdough and work the wood-fired oven. Toast, sweet pastries, pizzas and filled sandwiches. *7am-5pm, from 8am Sat & Sun*

Petit by Sam ⓖ
30 D4

Little patisserie using natural ingredients such as date puree, honey, and almond flour as alternatives to butter, refined sugar and white flour. Vegan, dairy- and gluten-free pick-me-ups. *9am-5pm Mon-Fri, 9.30am-5.30pm Sat & Sun*

Cafe Bites

Lavinia Good Food ⓖ
 31 C4

All-day healthy breakfasts, spelt mini-pizzas, smashed avocado on toast, apple pie and vegan brownies. (No cash.) *8.30am-4pm*

Mon-Fri, 9.30am-5pm Sat & Sun

Back to Black ⓖ
 32 C4

Ultra-cool neighbourhood cafe with teal walls and cakes, pies and powerballs baked in-house. The coffee here is also amazing – Back to Black roasts its own beans. *9am-6pm*

Soup, Salads & Sandwiches

Soup en Zo ⓖ
 33 C4

Steaming cups of soup changing daily in unusual flavour combos; spicy spinach and coconut or maybe potato with Roquefort. Takeaway only. *11am-8pm Mon-Fri, noon-7pm Sat & Sun*

SLA ⓖ
34 E3

Quick, well-priced healthy lunches from an Amsterdam chain. Salads and bowls loaded with organic veggies and ingredients like zucchini noodles and curry hummus. *11am-9pm*

Stach ⓖ
 35 C4

Popular deli branch of an Amsterdam favourite.

Gets crowded but is a great option for takeaway pastas, sandwiches and coffee. Grab your goodies to eat on a canal-side bench. *8am-10pm Mon-Sat, 9am-9pm Sun*

Van Dobben ⓖ
 36 E3

Fast-serving, affordable diner famous for *kroketten* (croquettes). Go for a finely sliced pork sandwich slathered in satay sauce. *10am-8pm Sun-Thu, to 9pm Fri & Sat*

Dutch Classics

De Carrousel ⓖ ⓖ
37 D5

Some of Amsterdam's best traditional large, thin Dutch pancakes (both sweet and savoury), as well as *poffertjes* (tiny pancakes topped with powdered sugar). *10am-7pm, to 8pm Sat & Sun*

De Blauwe Hollander ⓖ ⓖ
 38 B4

It's all *gezelligheid* (cosiness) and comfort food at this red-lamp-lit place with Dutch staples such as pea soup with bacon, and *stamppot* (veggie mash)

91

with pork sausage.
noon-10.30pm

Herengracht Restaurant & Bar € €
39 C2

A full selection of *borrel-hapjes* (fried bar snacks) including *bitterballen* (deep-fried croquettes with ragu filling) and *kaas-soufflé* (breaded and fried pastry filled with cheese). Perfect canal-side seating. *noon-midnight*

Bistros

Buffet van Odette € €
40 C4

Chef-restauranteur Odette serves decadent mains at her enchanting canal-side restaurant. Bookings are essential. *noon-3pm & 5.30-11pm Wed-Fri, from 11.30am Sat*

Zoldering € € €
41 F4

Michelin-starred bistro serving refined French-Dutch cuisine incorporating seasonal and foraged ingredients. The beautiful, 17th-century step-gabled building's interiors are also just *wow. 5.30-10pm Mon-Fri, from 4pm Sat*

Global Flavours

Salsa Shop €
42 F2

Create your own burritos, bowls and taco salads. The interior is modern and

simple; good for an easy stop near Rembrandtplein. *11.30am-10pm Sun-Thu, to 11pm Fri & Sat*

Bojo € €
43 B3

Cosied-up wooden tables embellished with colourful Indonesian décor for sizzling satay, filling fried rice and steaming bowls of noodle soup. Book ahead. *4-11pm*

Demetra € €
44 E2

Hidden down a quiet alley, this Italian eatery is a comfy place to unwind. Pizzas and pasta are served from an open kitchen. Look for the orange door. *5-10pm, to 9pm Sun*

Levant € € €
45 C5

Elegant Turkish eatery serving meze and grilled meats by candlelight. Reserve a spot on the back terrace right against the water. *5-11.30pm*

Drinking

Cocktail Bars

Door 74
46 D3

Innovative cocktails are served in a classy atmos-

phere. Themed cocktail lists change regularly. *8pm-3am Sun-Thu, to 4am Fri & Sat*

Flying Dutchmen Cocktails
47 C2

Monthly changing mixology and late service. It also has the Netherlands' largest backbar stocking over 900 different spirits. *5pm-4am*

Bruin Cafés

Café de Spuyt
48 B4

Amid the hubbub off busy Leidseplein, this is a mellow, friendly stop. Sip your way through the massive chalkboard menu of more than 150 Dutch and Belgian speciality beers. *4pm-3am Mon-Thu, 3pm-4am Fri & Sat*

Café de Wetering
49 C4

With a cascade of greenery draped over the outside, a cosy charmer for a drink or a snack, with a large fireplace and a gloriously faded interior that wouldn't look out of place in a Vermeer painting. *4pm-1am Mon-Thu, to 3am Fri, 3pm-2am Sat, 3pm-1am Sun*

Café Schiller
50 E3

Fabulous original Art Deco fittings such as

funky chandeliers and lamps shaped like thorny roses. Portraits of Dutch actors and cabaret artists from the 1920s and '30s line the walls, painted by the eponymous former owner. *3pm-1am Mon-Thu, 12.30pm-3am Fri & Sat, to 1am Sun*

Eijlders
 51 **A3**
Historic WWII meeting place for the Resistance, with waistcoated waiters and a low-key feel by day. It gets noisier at night, in keeping with its Leidse-plein surrounds. *4.30pm-1am Mon-Thu, noon-2am Fri & Sat, to 1am Sun*

Shopping

Design
Moooi
 52 **F4**
Gallery-shop founded by Dutch designers Marcel Wanders and Casper Vissers, featuring Dutch design at its most over-the-top, for instance a spun fibreglass chandelier, carbon-fibre chair, modular 'BFF sofa', life-size black horse lamp, or 'blow away vase' (a whimsical

twist on the classic Delft vase). *10am-6pm Thu-Sun*

Mobilia
53 **F4**
Dutch and international design is stunningly showcased at this three-storey 'lifestyle studio', with sofas, workstations, bookshelves, lighting, cushions, rugs and much more. *10am-6pm Tue-Sat*

Property Of...
54 **E3**
This Amsterdam-based label produces dapper travel gear, from backpacks to tote bags, using chrome-free leather and recycled materials. *11am-6.30pm*

Stationery & Music
Vlieger
55 **E2**
Since 1869, this two-storey shop has been supplying fancy paper: Egyptian papyrus, beautiful handmade papers from Asia and Central America, inlaid with petals, bamboo and more. *9am-6pm Mon, 9am-6pm Tue-Fri, 11am-5.30pm Sat*

MaisonNL
56 **F4**
Concept shop selling all sorts of beautiful things you didn't realise you needed, such as Christian

Lacroix notebooks and cute-as-a-button mouse toys in matchboxes by Maileg. *1-6pm Mon, 10am-6pm Tue-Sat, 1-5pm Sun*

Concerto
 57 **E4**
Established in 1955 and rambling over five floors, the Netherlands' largest music shop is audiophiles' heaven – snuggle into vinyl listening facilities or catch regular live sessions. *10am-6pm, from noon Sun & Mon*

Fashion
Shirt Shop
58 **D3**
On Amsterdam's main gay street, shop a kaleidoscopic array of shirts made for men not afraid of wearing colour: nice patterns, cool designs and funky motifs all from European collections. *1-7pm*

Skateboards Amsterdam
 59 **D3**
Everything required for the freewheeling lifestyle: cruisers, longboards, shortboards, electric and off-road boards, along with clothing essentials (Spitfire, Thrasher T-shirts and endless band shirts). *11am-6pm, from 1pm Sun & Mon*

See p114 for eating, drinking and shopping listings

Explore

Researched by
Catherine Le Nevez

Vondelpark, Oud-West & Oud-Zuid

At this neighbourhood's heart, the Vondelpark's rambling English-style gardens are strolling distance from the mega-museums of elegant Oud-Zuid and vibrant street life in and beyond Oud-West. The Vondelpark's 47 hectares of lawns, roses, sculptures, fountains, ponds and winding paths are where Amsterdammers flock on sunny days. Footsteps southeast, grassy square Museumplein is ringed by Amsterdam's biggest-hitting art museums. On the Vondelpark's northern side, cafes, restaurants, shops and bars line Overtoom and surrounding streets in the up-and-coming Oud-West, where converted tram sheds now house cultural and food hub De Hallen. Luxury boutiques and eateries grace the leafy streets to the Vondelpark's south.

Getting Around

 Cycling

Cycling is ideal for getting around this neighbourhood; it's especially handy for the more spread-out streets of Oud-West and within the Vondelpark itself.

 Tram

Tram 1 traverses Overtoom, 3 serves Concertgebouw, and 2, 3, 5 and 12 stop at Museumplein. Tram 5 continues to Amsterdam Zuid, which is linked by metro 52 to Centraal, and train to Centraal and the airport.

 Bus

Connexxion's Amsterdam Airport Express (bus 397; Niteliner N97) directly connects the airport with Museumplein.

Museumplein (p110)

SIPA USA/ALAMY

THE BEST

NATIONAL TREASURE CHEST
Rijksmuseum (p98)

VAN GOGH SHOWCASE
Van Gogh Museum (p102)

MODERN ART
Stedelijk Museum (p110)

PARK
Vondelpark (p106)

CULTURAL CENTRE
De Hallen (p113)

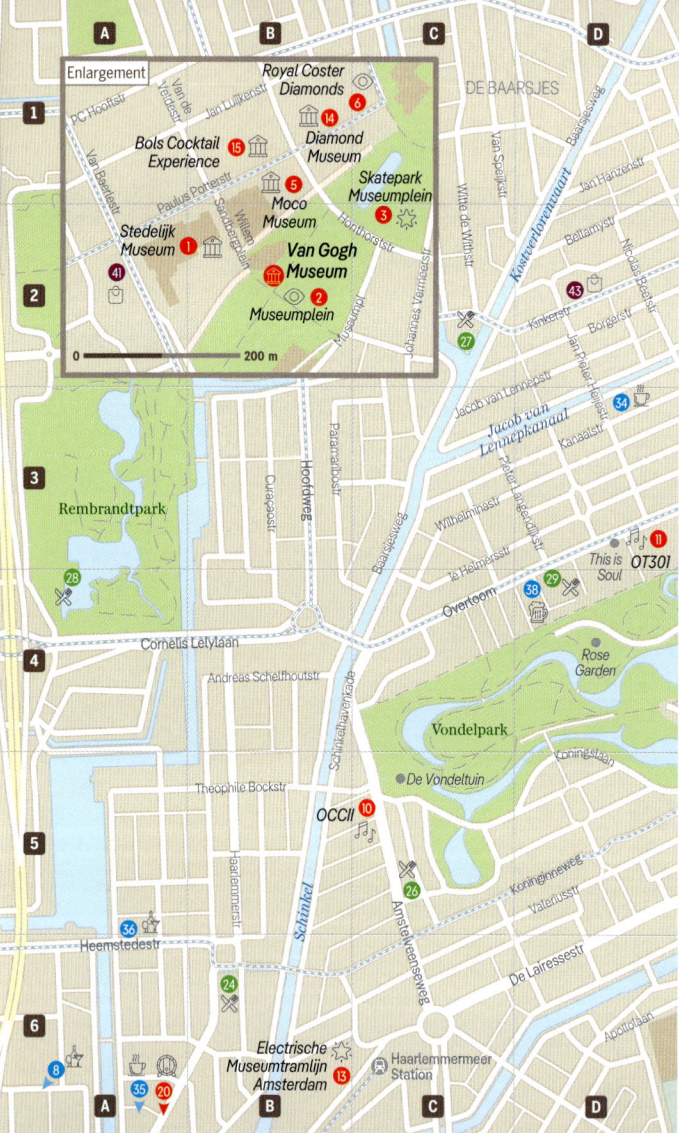

Enlargement

PC Hooftstr

Van de Veldestr

Jan Luijkenstr

DE BAARSJES

Royal Coster Diamonds

Van Speijkstr

Baarsjesweg

Bols Cocktail Experience 15

Diamond Museum 14 6

Jan Hanzenstr

Bellamystr

Paulus Potterstr

Moco Museum 5

Skatepark Museumplein 3

Kostverlorenvaart

Witte de Withstr

Nicolaas Beetsstr

Borgerstr

Van Beuerstr

Willem Sandbergplein

Stedelijk Museum 1

Van Gogh Museum

41

Museumplein 2

Museumstr

Johannes Vermeerstr

43

27

Kinkerstr

Jan Pieter Heijestr

34

0   200 m

Jacob van Lennepstr

Jacob van Lennepkanaal

Kanaalstr

Rembrandtpark

Hoofdweg

Curaçaostr

Baarsjesweg

Wilhelminastr

1e Helmersstr

Pieter Lastmankade

This is Soul

OT301 11

Paramaribostr

28

Cornelis Lelylaan

38 29

Overtoom

Rose Garden

Andreas Schelfhoutstr

Schinkelhavenkade

Vondelpark

De Vondeltuin

Koningslaan

Theophile Bockstr

OCCII 10

Haarlemmerstr

Schinkel

Amstelveenseweg

26

Koninginneweg

Valeriusstr

36

Heemstedestr

De Lairessestr

24

Apollolaan

Electrische Museumtramlijn Amsterdam

Haarlemmermeer Station

8

35 20

13

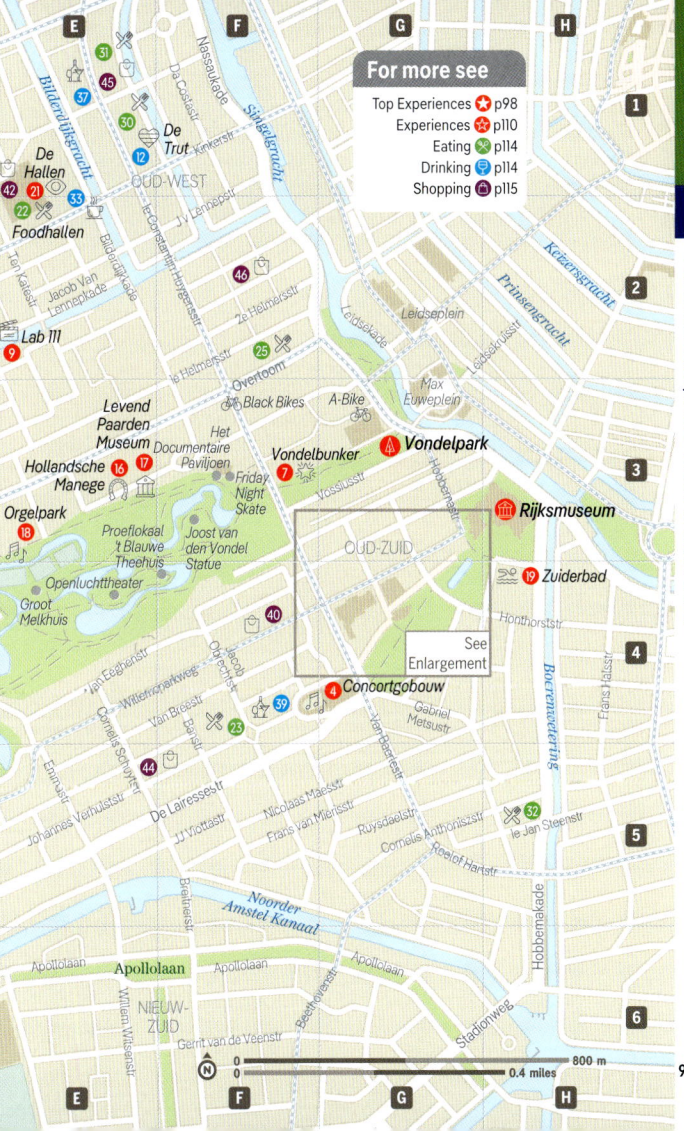

For more see

Top Experiences 🔴 p98
Experiences 🔴 p110
Eating 🟢 p114
Drinking 🔵 p114
Shopping 🟣 p115

E F G H

De Trut
De Hallen
OUD-WEST
Foodhallen

Lab 111

Levend Paarden Museum
Hollandsche Manege
Orgelpark

Proeflokaal 't Blauwe Theehuis
Joost van den Vondel Statue
Openluchttheater
Groot Melkhuis

Het Documentaire Paviljoen
Friday Night Skate

Black Bikes
A-Bike

Overtoom

Leidseplein
Leidsekade

Max Euweplein

⚠ **Vondelpark**

Vondelbunker

🏛 **Rijksmuseum**

OUD-ZUID

🏊 **Zuiderbad**

See Enlargement

🎵 **Concertgobouw**

Gabriel Metsustr

De Lairessestr
JJ Viottastr
Nicolaas Maesstr
Frans van Mierisstr
Ruysdaelstr
Cornelis Anthoniszstr
1e Jan Steenstr

Johannes Verhulststr

Noorder Amstel Kanaal

Apollolaan
Apollolaan
Apollolaan

NIEUW-ZUID

Gerrit van de Veenstr
Stadionweg

0 ————— 800 m
0 ————— 0.4 miles

Rijksmuseum

Resembling a castle, the turreted, red-brick Rijksmuseum is one of the world's most magnificent museums, and a fitting showcase for masterpieces by the nation's greatest artistic talent, such as Rembrandt, Vermeer and Van Gogh, displayed alongside some 8000 other treasures across 1.5km of gallery space.

MAP P96 **H3**

PLANNING TIP
While you can see the highlights in around two hours, the collection is huge; consider allowing much longer. Before noon and weekday afternoons from 3pm are usually quietest.

Scan this QR code for full opening hours and to book tickets.

History & Layout

Today's Rijksmuseum was more than two centuries in the making: the first museum conceived to hold national and royal collections opened in Den Haag's Huis Ten Bosch in 1800 (Jan Asselijn's *The Threatened Swan*, c 1650, was its first acquisition). During French rule, the collections moved to the new capital, opening on the top floor of Amsterdam's Royal Palace in 1809, where they were joined by paintings including Rembrandt's *The Night Watch*.

Following King Willem I's ascension to the throne, the collections moved locations until architect PJH (Petrus Josephus Hubertus; 'Pierre') Cuypers was chosen to design a purpose-built permanent home for the national museum. Its construction, incorporating neo-Gothic and Renaissance styles, began in 1876 and it opened in 1885.

Renovations have kept Cuypers' interior layout over four levels, from Floor 0, with its skylit atrium, up to Floor 3. Navigate via the museum's app.

Floor 2 Highlights

On the 2nd floor, the **Gallery of Honour** (pictured), with masterpieces spanning 1600 to 1700, is the best place to begin your visit. Among the masters here are Frans Hals; *The Merry Drinker* (1628–30) shows his broad, fluid brushstrokes. Beautiful works by Johannes (Jan) Vermeer featuring intimate, almost photographic-like domestic details include *The*

ERIK SMITS, VIA RIJKSMUSEUM

Milkmaid (1660; also called *The Kitchen Maid*) and *Woman in Blue Reading a Letter* (1663). Jan Steen depicted chaotic households to convey moral teachings, as in *The Merry Family* (1668).

Works by Rembrandt include his self-portrait as the Apostle Paul, and a couple's intimate caress in *The Jewish Bride* (1665). The Rijksmuseum's star is Rembrandt's colossal *The Night Watch* (1642). Originally titled *Archers under the Command of Captain Frans Banning Cocq*, it was later renamed due to a layer of grime that gave the mistaken impression it was set at night. It has since been restored to its original colours. The extensive research and conservation project Operation Night Watch has provided visitors the unique opportunity to witness it undergoing studies and repairs surrounded by a glass chamber; no completion date for the multiyear project is yet known but it remains in full public view.

TAKE A BREAK
The museum has a two espresso bars (plus another in the garden pavilion in summer) and an atrium cafe. Michelin-starred restaurant **Rijks** is accessible without a museum ticket.

OUTSIDE THE RIJKSMUSEUM

The building was envisaged as a city gateway, linking Amsterdam's historic core with the new residential areas to the south. Part of Cuypers' brief was the bicycle-path passage that runs through the centre of the building. It's free to stroll the museum's gardens amid the roses, hedges, fountains and a greenhouse. Major sculpture exhibitions take place here.

Splendid 17th-century treasures are displayed in rooms either side of the Gallery of Honour. On one side is delicate blue-and-white **Delftware pottery** from the late 1600s. The other features extraordinary **dollhouses**; merchant's wife Petronella Oortman employed carpenters, glassblowers and silversmiths to make items using the same materials as for full-scale versions.

Cuypers Library

From the 2nd-floor balcony, you can see the towering book-lined space of the **Cuypers Library,** one of the world's finest art libraries. Reservations are required for its reading room.

Floor 1 Highlights

Highlights on the 1st floor, spanning 1700 to 1900, include the Rijksmuseum's largest painting, Jan Willem Pieneman's *The Battle of Waterloo* (1824), **Van Gogh**'s famous 1887 *Self-portrait*, and a gilded, recreated 18th-century **Canal House Room**.

Floor 0 Highlights

Covering the years 1100 to 1600, the ground floor's Special Collections span magic lanterns, armoury, **ship models** and Dutch status symbols from previous eras, such as musical instruments and silver miniatures. Early gems include works by Dürer, and Charles V's cutlery.

The serene **Asian Pavilion**, a separate sandstone-and-glass structure that's often devoid of crowds, holds first-rate artworks from China, Indonesia, Japan, India, Thailand and Vietnam.

Floor 3 Highlights

The museum's top floor encompasses 1900 to the year 2000. Works here include paintings by Karel Appel, Constant Nieuwenhuys and fellow **CoBrA members** of the post-WWII movement, and **Dutch design** furniture.

RIJKSMUSEUM

Floor 3: 1900–2000

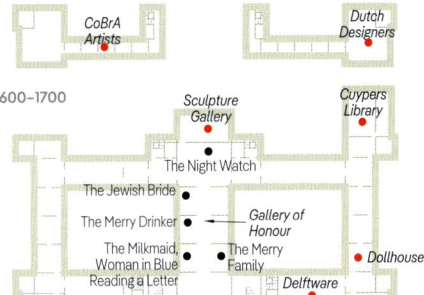

CoBrA
Artists

Dutch
Designers

Floor 2: 1600–1700

Sculpture
Gallery

Cuypers
Library

The Night Watch

The Jewish Bride

The Merry Drinker

Gallery of
Honour

The Milkmaid,
Woman in Blue
Reading a Letter

The Merry
Family

Dollhouses

Delftware

View of
Ambon

Great Hall

Floor 1: 1700–1900

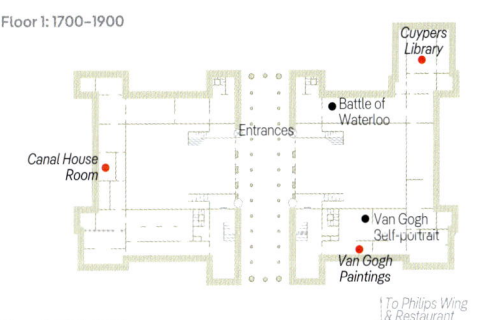

Cuypers
Library

Battle of
Waterloo

Entrances

Canal House
Room

Van Gogh
Self-portrait

Van Gogh
Paintings

To Philips Wing
& Restaurant

Floor 0: 1100–1600

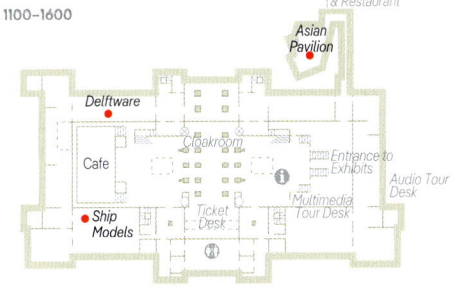

Asian
Pavilion

Delftware

Cloakroom

Entrance to
Exhibits

Cafe

Audio Tour
Desk

Ship
Models

Ticket
Desk

Multimedia
Tour Desk

★ **TOP EXPERIENCE**

Van Gogh Museum

Opened in 1973 to house the collection of Vincent Van Gogh's younger brother Theo, the Van Gogh Museum manages to feel personal and intimate, while containing the world's largest collection – some 200 paintings and 500 drawings – by Vincent and his contemporaries, including Gauguin and Monet.

MAP P96 **B2**

PLANNING TIP
Plan to spend around two hours at the museum (longer if you're a serious fan). Before 11am, after 3pm and Friday evenings are the quietest times to visit.

Scan this QR code for full opening hours and to book tickets.

Backstory

Vincent van Gogh died in 1890, aged 37, having only sold a single painting in his lifetime, leaving his prolific collection to his brother, Theo, who died the following year. Theo's widow, Jo van Gogh-Bonger, then left it on her death in 1925 to her son, Vincent Willem van Gogh, who loaned it to the Stedelijk Museum until the Dutch government commissioned this dedicated museum.

The 1973 building was designed by De Stijl architect Gerrit Rietveld. Kisho Kurokawa's glass exhibition wing (nicknamed 'the Mussel') was completed in 1999, and in 2015, an extension providing an additional 800 sq metres of space incorporated the striking entrance hall.

Layout

Spread over four levels, from the ground-level Floor 0 to Floor 3, the museum's chronological layout allows you to observe Van Gogh's work as it evolves from his early depictions of sombre countryfolk in the Netherlands to his iconic vivid, swirling landscapes in southern France. The individual paintings often move around depending on the current exhibition theme.

JAN KEES STEENMAN, VIA VAN GOGH MUSEUM AMSTERDAM

Visiting the Museum

Plan ahead as the museum gets booked out days in advance. Prepurchase timed-entry tickets online. Timeslots also need to be reserved even if you have a museum pass (note the I amsterdam City Card isn't valid here).

Check dates for 'Vincent on Friday' evening events (€11) with live performances, DJs and more.

The **information desk** can advise on treasure hunts and other activities for kids.

Collection Highlights

Van Gogh's earliest works are from his time in the Dutch countryside and studying at Antwerp's Royal Academy of Fine Arts. Peasant life is celebrated in many of his early works such as *The Potato Eaters* (1885).

TAKE A BREAK
Along with ground-floor cafes (in the atrium and next to the shop), **Bistro Vincent** has cuisine inspired by Van Gogh's paintings.

VAN GOGH'S LETTERS

What makes the museum so special is the intimate connection you experience with the artist – in addition to his paintings and drawings, it holds over 800 handwritten letters, mainly between Vincent and his brother Theo, as well as artists such as Paul Gauguin and Émile Bernard. The museum has categorised all of Van Gogh's letters online at *vangoghletters. org*.

After his father became pastor of the Dutch Reformed Church in Nuenen in 1882, Van Gogh stayed at the vicarage, and painted *Congregation Leaving the Reformed Church at Nuenen* (1884–85) in early 1884, which he modified in late 1885, painting out a peasant with a spade in the foreground and adding mourning clothes to the congregation, after his father's death earlier that year. The painting, along with *View of the Sea at Scheveningen* (1882), was stolen in 2002 and recovered in 2016.

In 1886, Van Gogh moved to Paris, where his brother Theo was working as an art dealer. Unable to pay for models, Vincent started painting multiple **self-portraits** to improve his portraiture techniques. He met some of the Impressionists, and his palette began to brighten.

Van Gogh headed south to Provence in 1888 to paint its colourful landscapes and intense Mediterranean light. *Sunflowers* (1889) dates from this period, as does *The Yellow House* (1888), a rendering of the property Van Gogh rented in Arles; *The Bedroom* (1888) depicts Van Gogh's sleeping quarters at the house. Paul Gauguin came to stay, but their artistic differences led to fierce arguments. It was here, in 1888, during a bout of psychosis, that Van Gogh sliced off part of his ear.

Van Gogh had himself committed to an asylum in Saint-Rémy in 1889, where he continued to paint with a wild, expressive fervour. The countryside's olive and cypress trees feature in his works, as do his famous *Irises*. In 1890, he returned north in France to Auvers-sur-Oise to be closer to Theo. The ominous *Wheatfield with Crows* (1890) was among his last works before his suicide.

Other Artists

The museum also holds works by Vincent's peers, including Gauguin, Monet and Toulouse-Lautrec. There are also paintings by Van Gogh's precursors as well as later artists Van Gogh influenced.

Van Gogh Museum

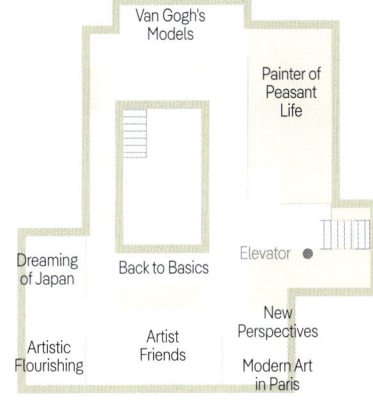

Floor 1

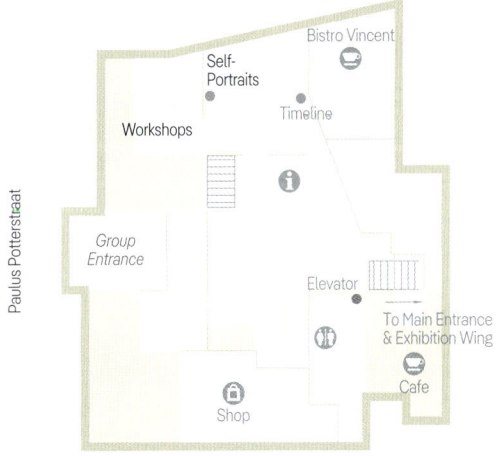

Floor 0

Vondelpark

Shaped somewhat like a cricket bat lying on its side, with the 'handle' pointing towards Leidseplein and the base on Amstelveenseweg, this elongated green space gets filled with picnickers, joggers, skaters and a constantly whizzing parade of bikes, but its spacious layout means it avoids feeling uncomfortably crowded.

MAP P96 **G3**

PLANNING TIP
The park is perfect for cycling away from road traffic – rent wheels nearby at **Black Bikes** (black -bikes.com) or **A-Bike** (a-bike. nl). On Overtoom, **This Is Soul** (thisissoul.com) hires in-line skates.

Scan this QR code for more information about visiting the Vondelpark.

Park History

Originally a private park for the wealthy only, these sprawling, English-style gardens were laid out on marshland and opened in 1865, and expanded between 1875 and 1877 to the current size. Although known as Nieuwe Park (New Park), in 1867 a statue of poet and playwright **Joost van den Vondel** (1587–1679) was created by sculptor Louis Royer. Locals began referring to the park as Vondelspark (Vondel's Park), which it was formally renamed. The fragrant **rose garden**, with some 70 different species, was added in 1936. Bought by the city council in 1953, the park finally opened to the public.

During the 1960s and '70s, Amsterdam became the *magisch centrum* (magic centre) of Europe. As hippies flocked here, a housing shortage saw speculators leaving buildings empty. Squatting (illegal since 2010) became widespread, and Dutch authorities turned the park into a temporary open-air dormitory. Although the sleeping bags are long gone today, an indie spirit persists.

After the Vondelpark was listed as a national monument in 1996, renovations incorporated an extensive drainage system to counteract it sinking while conserving its historic appearance.

WOLF·PHOTOGRAPHY/SHUTTERSTOCK

Birdlife

The Vondelpark is a haven for birdlife. Species such as coots, great spotted woodpeckers, herons, jackdaws, kingfishers, mallards, moorhens, mute swans, oystercatchers, parakeets, reed warblers, robins, sparrowhawks, tawny owls and wood-pigeons are commonly spotted, as well as white storks – look for stork poles with nests in spring.

Entertainment & Festivals

Open-air theatre the **Openluchttheater** *(openlucht theater.nl)* hosts free performances from Friday evenings to Sunday afternoons May to September. **Het Documentaire Paviljoen** *(idfa.nl)*, in the **Vondelparkpaviljoen** (pictured), is the home base of the citywide, fortight-long **IDFA** (International Documentary Film Festival Amsterdam) in November.

The pavilion is the departure point of the mass **Friday Night Skate** *(fridaynightskate.com)*.

TAKE A BREAK
Park refreshments include Brouwerij 't IJ taproom **Proeflokaal 't Blauwe Theehuis**; garden cafe **De Vondeltuin**; and Hansel-and-Gretel-like chalet **Groot Melkhuis**.

🚶 **WALKING TOUR**

Explore the Vondelpark, Oud-West & Oud-Zuid

While this area is home to chart-topping sights like the city's big three museums (the Rijksmuseum, Van Gogh Museum and Stedelijk Museum) and its favourite park (the greenery-filled Vondelpark), they're only a few steps from refreshingly untouristed backstreets. Discover a different side to the neighbourhood on this walk from Oud-West via the Vondelpark to Oud-Zuid.

START	END	LENGTH
Monks Coffee Roasters (tram 13/19 Bilderdijkstraat)	Museumplein (tram 2/5/12 Museumplein)	4.5km; 2hr

1 Coffee Shot

Oud-West has some of Amsterdam's best coffee and it doesn't come better than **Monks Coffee Roasters** on buzzing Bilderdijkstraat. It sources and roasts outstanding coffee, including a phenomenal house blend; the bare-boards space is brilliant for brunch.

2 Dutch Design

Inside cultural centre De Hallen (p113), the **Maker Store** showcases 80+ Amsterdam artisans, with handmade, sustainable items like screen-printed T-shirts and wallets made from old market-stall coverings, natural-dye fabrics, prints of hand-drawn illustrations of Amsterdam and jewellery made from recycled materials. On Saturdays and Sundays, meet the artisans at the Maker Market.

3 Market Browsing

The small yet thronged street market **Ten Katemarkt** brims with produce and daily essentials, every day except Sunday.

4 Picasso Sculpture

Enter the Vondelpark (p106). Along with ephemeral installations and artworks, permanent sculptures dotted through the park include Picasso's 6m-high abstract work *Figure découpée l'Oiseau* (*Bird Cut Out*; 1965), commonly known as **The Fish**, which he donated for the park's centenary on the condition it remain here.

5 Architectural Church

Exit the Vondelpark. On its northern edge, the neo-Gothic cross-basilica **Vondelkerk** was designed in 1872 by Pierre Cuypers (of Rijksmuseum and Centraal Station fame).

6 Little Woodcutter

Hidden up in the Leidsebosje parkland, a 50cm-high bronze sculpture **Boomzagertje** ('little woodcutter') leaning over and sawing a branch with both hands was first installed by an anonymous artist in 1989 and, after the original branch was sawn off, was relocated in 2020 to an adjacent tree (nearest to Stromma's bar-cafe).

7 Ritzy Shopping

Window-shop along boutique-lined **PC Hooftstraat**, Amsterdam's ritziest shopping street, which queues up ultra-luxe shops like Cartier, Dior, Louis Vuitton, Tiffany & Co and Versace along its length.

8 Monumental Square

Amsterdam's most famous museums cluster around **Museumplein**, a vast public square that was laid out to host the World Exhibition in 1883, named when the Rijksmuseum opened two years later. It's now a hub where everyone picnics on the lawns when the weather warms up. Markets, concerts, festivals and some of Amsterdam's biggest celebrations take place here throughout the year.

EXPERIENCES

View Modern Art
MUSEUM

MAP: **1** P96 **B2**

The fabulous **Stedelijk Museum** (*stedelijk.nl; adult/child €22.50/ free*) is an impressive, light, bright modern art museum, displaying artworks from its 90,000-strong collection dating from 1870 onwards. Of the Stedelijk's vast repository, some 500 works are displayed in the permanent collection presentation at any one time. While it rotates, you're likely to see works by Monet, Picasso, Kandinsky, Matisse, Chagall, Warhol, Rothko, De Kooning and more. It's housed in a gabled, red-brick, Dutch Renaissance–style masterpiece designed by Amsterdam city architect AM (Adriaan Willem) Weissman in 1895; temporary installations of the latest in contemporary art show in its 2012-opened wing known as 'the Bathtub' (for reasons that are immediately apparent).

The entrance incorporates the Don Quixote Sculpture Hall, showcasing works by sculptors such as Henry Moore, Anne Imhof and Damien Hirst. There's free access (no ticket required) when the museum's open, and after-hours views of the illuminated sculptures.

Skate at Museumplein
PARK

More than just a park for relaxing and for attending celebrations and major events (like Amsterdam's main New Year's Eve fireworks), **Museumplein** (MAP: **2** P96 **C2**) is also home to a state-of-the-art **skatepark** (MAP: **3** P96 **C2**) for skateboarders, BMXers and in-line skaters; it's open 24 hours, with lighting until 10pm. Ice skating has taken place here since 1864; a picturesque ice rink sets up each winter.

Appreciate Exceptional Acoustics
CONCERT HALL

MAP: **4** P96 **G4**

One of Museumplein's trio of late-19th-century architectural beauties, along with the Stedelijk and Rijksmuseum, Amsterdam's magnificent concert hall the **Concertgebouw** (*concertgebouw.nl; ticket prices vary*) was built for its 1888 debut by AL (Adolf Leonard; 'Dolf') van Gendt, who engineered its near-perfect acoustics. Former Royal Concertgebouw Orchestra conductor Bernard Haitink remarked that the world-famous hall was the orchestra's best instrument.

The home of the Netherlands Philharmonic and the Netherlands Chamber Orchestra, it presents a wide-ranging programme. In addition to the 1974-capacity Grote Zaal (main hall) and 437-seat Kleine Zaal (recital hall), the 150-capacity Koor Zaal (choir hall) is often used as a jazz club.

From September to June, free half-hour concerts take place at 12.30pm on Wednesdays (arrive early), with discounted concerts from 11am to noon on Sundays.

Go Moco

MAP: **5** P96 **B1**

MUSEUM

Overlooking Museumplein's northwestern corner from Honthorststraat, the Villa Alsberg, a beautiful 1904 villa designed by architect Eduard Cuypers, cousin of Rijksmuseum architect Pierre Cuypers, has been converted into the **Moco Museum** *(mocomuseum. com; adult/child from €17.95/15.95, with canal cruise from €35, with Heineken Experience from €40)* for 'Modern Contemporary', an independent museum founded by couple Lionel and Kim Logchies – private collectors and curators, who opened it in 2016. Its collection includes modern, contemporary, digital, immersive and street art by artists such as Andy Warhol, Keith Haring, Damien Hirst, Jeff Koons and Banksy. Sculptures displayed in the garden include a giant red gummy bear by artist WhIsBe (for 'What is Beauty') and outsized rocking horse by Dutch designer Marcel Wanders. Temporary exhibitions run in parallel throughout the year.

Visit the World's Oldest Working Diamond Factory

FACTORY

Just off Museumplein, 1840-founded **Royal Coster Diamonds** (MAP: **6** P96 **C1**; *royalcoster.com; guided tour/ private tour/Royal Experience/ masterclass free/€5/22.50/475)* is the oldest working diamond factory in the world. On free 30-minute guided tours, you can watch craftspeople cut and polish rough stones into

BEST COUNTERCULTURAL & NIGHTLIFE SPACES

Vondelbunker
MAP: **7** P96 **F3**
Music, film, poetry and more in a 1947 fallout shelter. *vondelbunker.nl*

Radion
MAP: **8** P96 **A6**
Former dental centre home to Amsterdam's techno scene; 24-hour clubbing. *radion.amsterdam*

Lab 111
MAP: **9** P96 **E2**
Once a university science laboratory, now a cinema screening cult films. *lab111.nl*

OCCII
MAP: **10** P96 **C5**
Legalised squat with an alternative scene from folk to punk. *occii.org*

OT301
MAP: **11** P96 **D3**
Street-art-covered ex-squat hosting an eclectic roster of bands, DJs, theatre and workshops. *ot301.nl*

De Trut
MAP: **12** P96 **E1**
Once-squatted printing machine factory that's a decades-strong volunteer-run LGBTIQ+ club famed for its Sunday parties. *trutfonds.nl*

sparkling gems while learning about the origins of diamonds and assessing their quality and value.

TRAM MUSEUM ON THE MOVE

Not a museum in a static sense, the **Electrische Museumtramlijn Amsterdam** (MAP: **13** P96 B6; *museum tramlijn.org; Heritage Line adult/child return €7.50/5, City Tour adult/child €10/5*) gives you the opportunity to travel on historic trams from the Netherlands, Austria and Poland collected between the 1950s and '70s – the earliest date back to the 1890s. On Sundays from April to October, the Heritage Line (Line 30) departs from red-brick Haarlemmermeer Station near the Vondelpark to Amstelveen via Amsterdamse Bos. A return trip takes about 1¼ hours; you can hop off at scheduled stops en route. Check for City Tour routes and special trips like winter illuminations.

The neighbouring **Diamond Museum** (MAP: **14** P96 B1; *diamond museum.com*) delves deeper into the history of diamonds in Amsterdam.

Mix Cocktails

MUSEUM

MAP: **15** P96 B1

Local institution Bols, the world's oldest distilled spirit brand, has been distilling liqueurs in Amsterdam since 1575. You can taste them during an hour-long audio-guided tour of the **Bols Cocktail Experience** (*bols.com; tour €19.50, with 30-minute/one-hour cocktail workshop €34.50/46.50*), getting to grips with the tools, glass shapes, ice and different aromas (atomisers cover an entire wall) to construct and shake your own cocktail. Minimum age is 18.

Be Whisked Back in Time at a Neoclassical Riding School

HORSE RIDING, MUSEUM

The grandiose indoor riding school **Hollandsche Manege** (Dutch Riding School; MAP: **16** P96 E3; *deholland schemanege.nl; museum adult/child €12.50/8.50, high tea €34.95, 30-minute riding/side-saddle lesson €49/55, one-hour riding lesson €77.50*) was inspired by Vienna's famous Spanish Riding School.

Built in 1882 by architect AL van Gendt, the neoclassical building retains its charming horsehead facade and is a national monument. Its **Levend Paarden Museum** (Living Horse Museum; MAP: **17** P96 E3), closed Mondays, details the building's history alongside the 'world of the horse' through equine art and displays including historic riding equipment.

A highlight is watching a balletic carousel display with women riding side-saddle (seated with both legs to the horse's left side) and men riding to the right, which has Dutch Intangible Cultural Heritage designation.

It's also possible for visitors to book ahead for one-off 30-minute or hour-long standard private **riding lessons** at its arena.

Listen to Organ Music in a Former Church
CONCERT VENUE

MAP: **18** P96 **E3**

Originally known as the Parkkerk for its position on the edge of the Vondelpark, the **Orgelpark** *(orgel park.nl; adult/child from €20/12.50)* occupies a 1918 late neo-Renaissance brick church designed by Dutch architect EAC (Ernst Adolph Christiaan) Roest. Around 80 events take place each year, including classical and jazz, along with combined performances with other artistic forms like film or dance – check the agenda online.

Splash in an Exquisite Swimming Pool
SWIMMING POOL

MAP: **19** P96 **H4**

Originally the Velox cycling school, dating from 1897, this building behind the Rijksmuseum on Hobbemastraat was converted in 1912 into a beguilingly splendid public pool, the **Zuiderbad** *(amsterdam .nl/zuiderbad; swimming €5.50, wellness facilities €3.30)*. It's a grand edifice restored to its original glory, full of tiles (including the beautiful fountain with Amsterdam's city symbol 'XXX'), original wooden changerooms and underwater lighting. There are steam cabins and herbal baths. The schedule for swimming *(recreatiezwemmen in diep water)* varies daily; check it online.

Distil Rum
DISTILLERY

MAP: **20** P96 **A6**

In the trendy neighbourhood of Hoofddorppleinbuurt, you can distil your own rum. During a 90-minute distilling workshop and tour at **Spirited Union Rum Company** *(spirited-union.com; distilling workshop & tour €70)*, you get to check out the production facility and create your own 70cL bottle using one of four rums as bases, then choose your botanicals (pineapple, grapefruit, cacao, cinnamon, coconut or coffee) in your own copper still. Workshops and tours include a tasting.

Head to Oud-West's Food & Cultural Hub
CULTURAL CENTRE

Cavernous red-brick sheds built to service Amsterdam's trams from 1901 were converted a century later into an impressive food hall and cultural complex, electrifying the surrounding Oud-West.

De Hallen (MAP: **21** P96 **E1**; *dehallen -amsterdam.nl*) incorporates sustainable Dutch design and fashion boutiques, an antiques shop, a bike seller-repairer, a hairdressing academy-salon, a library, galleries, a nine-screen cinema, **Filmhallen**, and a hotel.

At De Hallen's heart, its skylit food hall, **Foodhallen** (MAP: **22** P96 **E2**), is an airy, open-plan communal dining area surrounded by 21 stands cooking everything from Mumbai street food to Dutch-speciality meatballs.

Regular events include DJs, live music, markets, sustainability workshops and pop-up exhibitions.

Best Places for...

⑥ Budget **⑥⑥** Midrange **⑥⑥⑥** Top End

See p96 for map of locations

EXPLORE

VONDELPARK, OUD-WEST & OUD-ZUID

Eating

Classic Dutch

Visque Winkel ⑥
23 F4

Fishmonger with ready-to-eat *kibbeling* (small fried fish pieces), seafood sandwiches, smoked eel and herring. *noon-6pm Mon, 8am-6pm Tue-Fri, 9am-5pm Sat*

Lunchroom Grannies ⑥
24 B6

Dutch favourites for breakfast, eg *chocoladebroodje* (chocolate sprinkles on bread) as well as lunch, like *limburgse stoof* (stew). *9am-5pm Wed-Sun*

Hap Hmm ⑥ ⑥
25 F2

Comfort food since 1935, from grandmother's recipe meatballs to chicken casserole, schnitzel, and pancakes or rhubarb pudding for dessert. *5-9.15pm Mon-Fri*

Gastronomy

Ron Gastrobar ⑥ ⑥ ⑥
26 C5

Casual fine-dining (and Michelin-starred) 'gastro-bar', with gourmet tapas-style dishes, dry-aged rib steaks and stellar seafood. *noon-10.30pm*

Daalder ⑥ ⑥ ⑥
27 C2

Menus (set and à la carte) are as artistic as the neon-lit, street-art-style dining room decor. *6.30-midnight Wed & Thu, 12.30-4.30pm & 6.30-midnight Fri & Sat*

Bolenius ⑥ ⑥ ⑥
28 A4

Waterside restaurant with Michelin red and green stars, and produce harvested from on-site greenhouse and gardens. *noon-3pm & 6-10pm Tue-Fri, 6.30-10.30pm Sat*

Vegan

Alchemist Garden ⑥
29 D4

This bright, high-ceilinged cafe's menu features dishes like almond-cheese and courgette quiche, and semolina and spinach lasagne. *9am-9pm Mon-Sat, noon-9pm Sun*

Soil ⑥ ⑥
30 E1

Fermentation, curing and smoking techniques are used in mushroom *bitter-ballen*, (deep-fried croquettes) miso-marinated tempeh burgers and other innovations, alongside natural wines. *noon-10pm Mon-Sat, to 9pm Sun*

Meatless District ⑥ ⑥
31 E1

Industrial-style space with classy dishes like braised artichoke with lemon aioli, Korean fried cauliflower and watermelon sashimi, and amazing cocktails. *5.30-10pm Wed-Mon*

Old Soul ⑥ ⑥
32 H5

Daily changing Surinamese vegan dishes such as yam and fried plantains; stuffed bitter melon and jackfruit stew; and sweet potato and peanut soup. *5-10pm Wed-Sun*

Drinking

Coffee

LOT61
33 E2

See (and smell) beans being roasted on the Probat in the open cellar. All coffees are double shots (unless you specify otherwise). *8am-6pm Mon-Fri, 9am-6pm Sat & Sun*

Trakteren
 D3

Preparation methods of single-origin beans at this specialist spot include Aeropress, V60 pour-over, Chemex, syphon and cold press. *8am-5pm Mon-Fri, 9am-5pm Sat*

Stean's Beans
 A6

Only a glass window separates the roastery from the cafe at this fabulous Hoofddorppleinbuurt space. *10.30am-4pm Mon, 9am-4pm Tue-Fri*

Bars
Lokaal van de Stad
 A5

Opening to an awesome Hoofddorppleinbuurt canal-side terrace, serving only Amsterdam craft brews. *8.30am-1am Sun-Thu, to 2am Fri & Sat*

Karavan
 E1

Opens to a huge beer garden that gets packed on sunny days, serving beers, natural wines, cocktails, mocktails and homemade sodas. *9am-1am Sun-Thu, to 3am Fri & Sat*

Craft & Draft
 D4

Over 40 beers rotating on the taps and 100 more

by the bottle. Try house collaborations with Netherlands brewers. *4pm-midnight Sun-Thu, to 2am Fri & Sat*

Welling
 F4

Tucked behind the Concertgebouw, this wood-panelled *bruin café* (traditional pub) often hosts live music by jazz musicians after their gigs. *4pm-1am Mon-Fri, 3pm-1am Sat & Sun*

Shopping

Fashion
Donsje
 F4

Adorable and environmentally friendly handmade booties, jumpsuits, trousers, cardigans, jackets and backpacks with nature themes. *10am-6pm Mon-Sat, to 5pm Sun*

Floris van Bommel
 A2

Brogues, loafers, sneakers, moccasins and boots by this 9th-generation-run shoemaker established in 1718. *10am-6pm Tue, Wed, Fri & Sat, to 7pm Thu, noon-6pm Sun & Mon*

Denim City
 E1

Stocks start-up labels' latest collections, recycles

denim into original pieces and does repairs. *11am-5pm Mon-Fri, to 6pm Sat, noon-6pm Sun*

Gekaapt
 D2

Permanent address of pop-up stores founded by young Amsterdam entrepreneurs and designers with an emphasis on sustainability. *11am-6pm Mon-Fri, 10am-6pm Sat, noon-5pm Sun*

Food & Drink
Nixx
 E5

Has a superb range of Dutch cheeses, roasts nuts in store, and sells dried fruit and natural wines. *9am-6.30pm Mon-Sat, noon-5pm Sun*

Cane & Grain
 E1

Specialises in *jenevers* (Dutch gin) and Caribbean rums, and organises tastings and workshops. *noon-6pm Tue, Wed & Sun, 11am-7pm Thu-Sat*

Little Plant Pantry
46 **F2**

Amsterdam's first zero-waste shop, with whole foods, a food counter with ready-to-eat dishes and artisan products like cotton bags. *11am-7pm Wed-Sat, to 6pm Sun*

See p130
for eating,
drinking and
shopping
listings

Explore
De Pijp & Zuid

Researched by
Catherine Le Nevez

EXPLORE

DE PIJP & ZUID

An island linked to surrounding districts by 16 bridges, De Pijp's straight, narrow streets reflect the stems of old clay pipes (hence 'the Pipe'). The city expanded here in the 19th century, when tenement blocks were rapidly constructed to relieve pressure on the Jordaan and provide cheap worker housing. In the 1960s and '70s, when many residents relocated for more space, the government refurbished the properties for immigrants. Artists, creatives, university students and entrepreneurs all flocked here, and gentrification took off, but it retains a village atmosphere, and is the gateway to lesser-visited areas and under-the-radar sights across Amsterdam Zuid (Amsterdam South).

Getting Around

Ⓜ Metro
Metro line M52 has stations at De Pijp, Europaplein and its southern terminus, Amsterdam Zuid.

🚋 Tram
Tram 24 rolls north–south from Centraal Station along Ferdinand Bolstraat. Tram 4 travels from Centraal via Rembrandtplein to De Pijp. Tram 3 traverses De Pijp between the Vondelpark and Oost. Tram 12 from Centraal via Leidseplein cuts through De Pijp and Rivierenbuurt.

🚌 Bus
Connexxion *(connexxion.nl)* buses serve some further-flung sights (I amsterdam City Cards and GVB transport tickets/passes aren't valid).

★

THE BEST

STREET MARKET
Albert Cuypmarkt (p126)
———
PICNIC TURF
Sarphatipark (p126)
———
INTERACTIVE TOUR
Heineken Experience (p120)
———
PARK
Amstelpark (p128)
———
FOREST
Amsterdamse Bos (p122)

Albert Cuypmarkt (p126)
XANDRA R/SHUTTERSTOCK

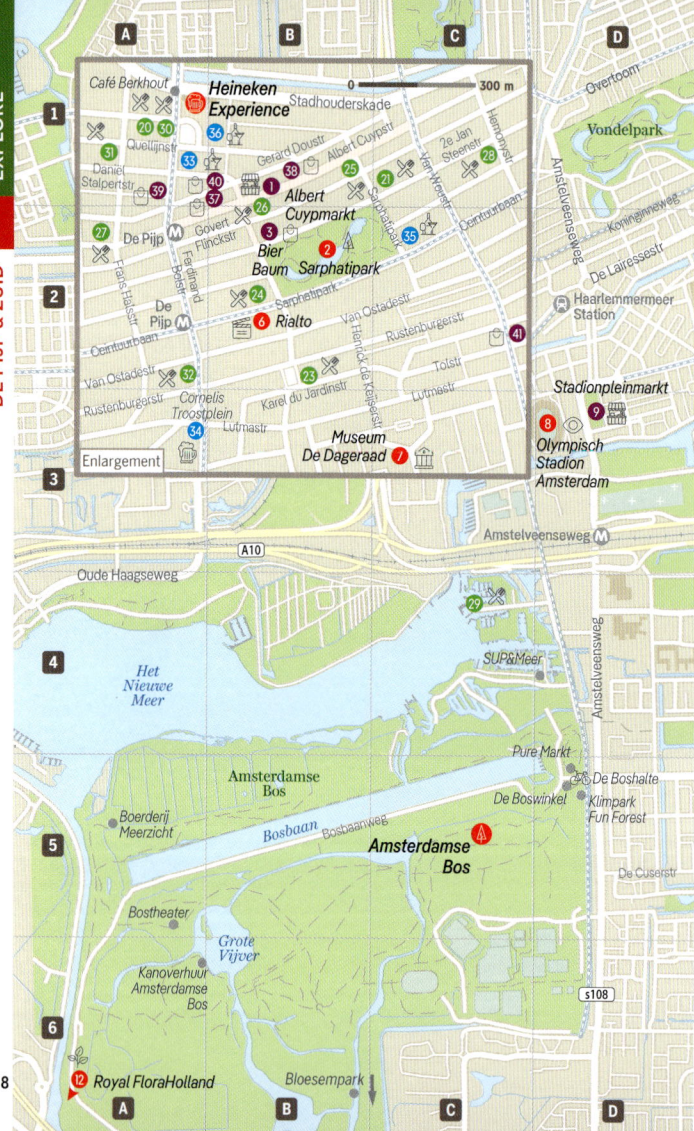

Café Berkhout

Heineken
Experience
Stadhouderskade

Quellijnstr

Daniel
Stalperstr

Gerard Doustr

De Pijp

Govert
Flinckstr

Albert
Cuypmarkt

Bier
Baum

Sarphatipark

Albert Cuypstr

De
Pijp

Sarphatipark

Rialto

Van Ostadestr

2e Jan
Steenstr

Van Woustr

Centuurbaan

Hendrick de Keijserstr

Rustenburgerstr

Tolstr

Lutmastr

Cornelis
Troostplein

Karel du Jardinstr

Lutmastr

Museum
De Dageraad

Enlargement

Van Ostadestr

Rustenburgerstr

300 m

Overtoom

Vondelpark

Amstelveenseweg

Koninginneweg

De Lairessestr

Haarlemmermeer
Station

Stadionpleinmarkt

Olympisch
Stadion
Amsterdam

Amstelveenseweg

A10

Oude Haagseweg

Het
Nieuwe
Meer

SUP&Meer

Amstelveenseweg

Amsterdamse
Bos

Bosbaan

Bosbaanweg

Amsterdamse
Bos

Pure Markt

De Boswinkel

De Boshalte

Klimpark
Fun Forest

De Cuserstr

Boerderij
Meerzicht

Bostheater

Grote
Vijver

Kanoverhuur
Amsterdamse
Bos

s108

Royal FloraHolland

Bloesempark

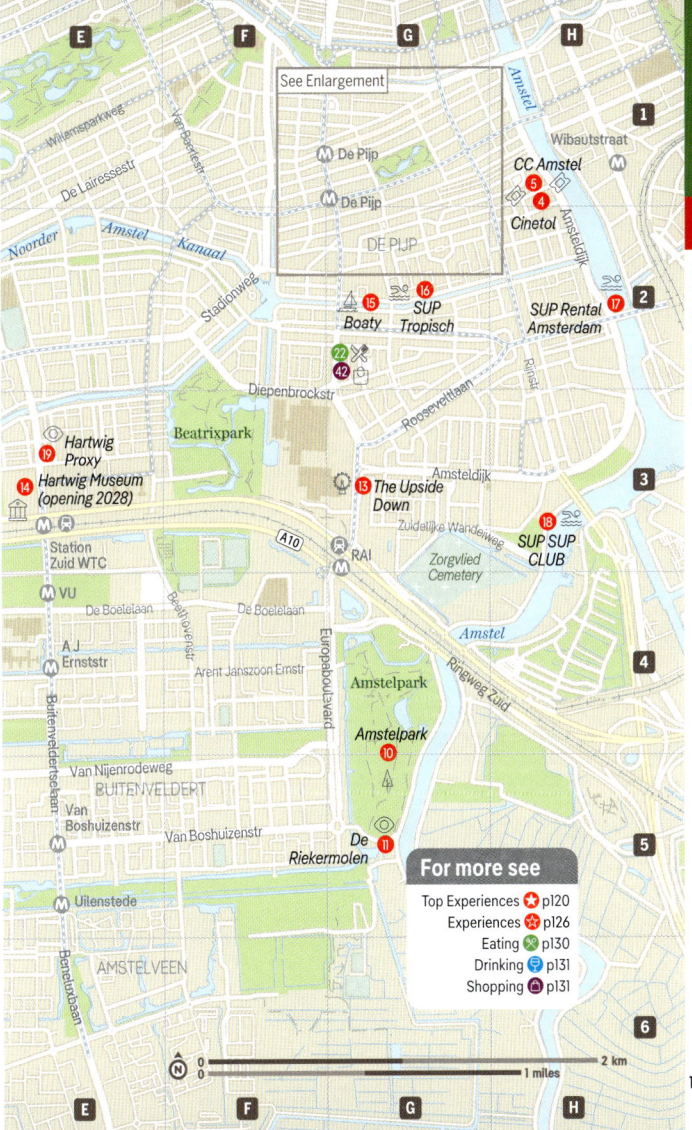

See Enlargement

De Pijp

De Pijp

DE PIJP

Willemsparkweg

De Lairessestr

Noorder   Amstel   Kanaal

Stadionweg

Wibautstraat

CC Amstel

Cinetol

Amsteldijk

Boaty   SUP
Tropisch

SUP Rental
Amsterdam

Diepenbrockstr

Roosevelttaan

Beatrixpark

Hartwig
Proxy

Hartwig Museum
(opening 2028)

The Upside
Down

Amsteldijk

A10   RAI

Station
Zuid WTC

VU

Zuidelijke Wandelweg

Zorgvlied
Cemetery

SUP SUP
CLUB

A J
Ernststr

De Boelelaan   De Boelelaan

Arent Janszoon Ernst

Amstel

Ringweg Zuid

Buitenveldertsehaan

Van Nijenrodeweg

BUITENVELDERT

Amstelpark

Van
Boshuizenstr   Van Boshuizenstr

Uilenstede

Amstelpark

AMSTELVEEN

Benderbaan

De
Riekermolen

For more see

Top Experiences p120
Experiences p126
Eating p130
Drinking p131
Shopping p131

0   2 km
0   1 miles

⭐ **TOP EXPERIENCE**

Heineken Experience

Since it began brewing in Amsterdam in 1864, Heineken has become a global juggernaut: upwards of 25 million serves of its pilsner are drunk daily worldwide. Production at its old De Pijp brewery ceased in 1988 but it's been repurposed as the whizz-bang, multisensory Heineken Experience.

MAP P118 **A1**

PLANNING TIP
Book tickets with timeslot entry online. The world's only official brand store, the on-site Heineken Flagship Store, filled with bar gadgets, coasters, T-shirts and more, is accessible without a ticket.

Scan this QR code for full opening hours and information on booking.

Heineken Tours

High spirited 90-minute self-guided tours start out by giving you an understanding of the company's heritage and the evolution of its distinctive translucent green bottles and red star logo. You'll then see the original gleaming copper vats, and experience the brewing process from the inside out as you're immersed in the production process via some 360-degree multimedia wizardry. Tours include two complimentary cold beers. True beer connoisseurs will shudder but the process is a lot of fun.

Upgraded tour options include the highly worthwhile two-hour Rooftop Experience. This allows visitors to discover the former malt attic, check out innovations like foam infusions and even taste test experimental brews at the Heineken Studio. Finish up by sipping an additional free beer while admiring the incredible panoramic views of Amsterdam from the terrace. True Heineken devotees also have the option of booking a 2½-hour VIP tour with a personal guide, five beers and food pairings.

HEINEKEN EXPERIENCE

Canal Cruises

It's also possible to combine a tour with a cruise on the city's waterways. Rock the City tours include a 45-minute canal cruise in a Heineken-bedecked covered boat (pictured), which departs from the canal directly out front.

Alternatively, you can book an hour-long Flagship Cruise on a smaller Heineken-branded open-topped sloop boat. While sailing Amsterdam's canals, guides offer insight into the city's culture, landmarks and history. Boats depart from near the Rijksmuseum, just a 15-minute walk away. Both options include an extra two beers, with more sold onboard.

TAKE A BREAK

Enjoy more Heineken, and great burgers, at timber-lined **Café Berkhout** across the street. For a change from beer, head to **Barça** (p131) for Spanish wines and Catalan cuisine.

EXPLORE

DE PIJP & ZUID

Amsterdamse Bos

On the city's southwestern edge, this activity-filled forest offers an accessible escape to the countryside. Planted from 1934 to provide employment during the Great Depression, Amsterdamse Bos (Amsterdam Forest) sprawls over 1000 hectares of *polder* (drained land) now alive with woodland, meadows, lakes and waterways.

MAP P118 **C5**

PLANNING TIP
Amsterdamse Bos is served by Connexxion buses (lines 178, 257 and 357) and, on Sundays from April to October, vintage trams run by the Electrische Museumtramlijn Amsterdam (p112).

Scan this QR code for full opening hours and information on booking.

Visitor Facilities

One of Europe's largest city parks (triple the size of New York's Central Park), the forest is vast: stop first at its visitors centre **De Boswinkel** for maps and tickets for 90-minute boat cruises (€10) on Wednesdays and Saturdays from May to September.

Across from De Boswinkel, bike-hire outlet **De Boshalte** (*deboshalte.com; bicycle hire per hour/day from €6/10*), closed Tuesdays, rents a huge range of wheels for adults and kids.

Forest Adventures

Over 50km of cycling trails thread through the forest, which is also laced with walking trails (routes range from 4km to 9km), and 21.5km of bridleways.

The **Klimpark Fun Forest** (*funforest.nl/amsterdam; adult/child from €32/23*) has 10 different rope courses and ziplining through the trees.

Water activities include swimming areas at the Grote Vijver ('great pond'), where you'll also find kids' paddling pools and canoe and pedal-boat rental at **Kanoverhuur Amsterdamse Bos** (*kanoverhuur-adam.nl; canoe/pedal boat per hour from €9/15*). On the Nieuwe Meer ('new lake'), **SUP&Meer** (*supenmeer.nl; SUP per 90 mins from €18*) rents SUPs and offers lessons.

Children can feed baby goats with bottles of milk in springtime at working organic goat farm

FOKKE BAARSSEN/SHUTTERSTOCK

De Ridammerhoeve *(geitenboerderij.nl; farm breakfast adult/child €16.80/12.85, cheese-making workshop €69.50, goat yoga €25.95)*, always closed on Tuesdays, plus Mondays from October to March.

From around mid- to late March, the **Bloesempark** (pictured) is another idyllic picnic spot when 400 Japanese cherry trees burst into blossom.

Entertainment

From July to September, the open-air **Bostheater** *(bostheater.nl)* stages everything from concerts and film screenings to plays (actors pause for planes to and from nearby Schiphol Airport). Check the programme and buy tickets online (arrive early for the best seats).

Hundreds of events are held throughout the year, from artisanal **Pure Markt** *(puremarkt.nl)* to festivals for food, wine, film, EDM, techno, folk, dragon boat races, canoe sprints and more; check *amsterdamsebos.nl/boskalender*.

QUICK BREAK
Farmhouse **Boerderij Meerzicht** *(boerde rijmeerzicht.nl)*, open Wednesday to Sunday, is a forest favourite for its animals (deer, peacocks and ponies), playgrounds and huge pancakes.

WALKING TOUR

Discover De Pijp

On this stroll along De Pijp's streets, many of which are named for painters and precious stones, you'll pass colourful public artworks and vestiges of its history as a diamond centre that give you a sense of the art and artistry that's at the heart and soul of this vibrant and creative neighbourhood.

START	END	LENGTH
Royal Asscher HQ (metro De Pijp)	*Wake Me Up When I'm Famous* (metro De Pijp)	2.1km; 1hr

1 Diamond Centre

Start in De Pijp's Diamantbuurt ('Diamond neighbourhood'), where the 1854-established diamond company retains its 1907-built **Royal Asscher HQ** in the castle-like main tower; its former factory now houses luxury apartments.

2 Glass Art

On the residential facades around Dora Tamanaplein and Cullinanplein, look for nine small diamond-like glass sculptures collectively known as **Revisiting the Cullinans** by Sanja Medić (2023). In 1908, Asscher cut the 3106-carat Cullinan, the world's largest gem-quality rough diamond, into nine stones for the British royal family's crown jewels.

3 Goblin House

Trace the Amstel north; at Ceintuurbaan 251's 1884 neo-Gothic mansion **Huis met de Kabouters**, look up to the elaborately carved wooden gables to see two cheeky lime-green goblin sculptures dressed in red hats and shorts, one holding a red ball and the other reaching to catch it.

4 Delftware Street Art

Further north, you'll come to the short, narrow tree-lined street **Hemonylaan**. Works of blue-and-white Delftware-style street art by stencil artist Hugo Kaagman decorate several walls and an electricity building.

5 Music Statue

Head along Albert Cuypstraat, home to the Albert Cuypmarkt (p126); on the corner of 1e Sweelinckstraat is a bronze **statue of André Hazes**, the *levenslied* (sentimental Dutch-language folk music) singer, who was born in De Pijp. Hazes' 1988 song 'Wij Houden van Oranje' (We Love Orange) was a hit when the Netherlands won that year's European Championships and remains a Dutch sporting anthem.

6 De Pijp's Pipes

Nearby on Gerard Douplein, you'll see **Drie Zuilen**, Henk Duijn's 1993 sculpture of three twisted ceramic 'pipes' referencing the neighbourhood's name.

7 Artist Square

Part of De Pijp's Heineken brewery once stood at **Marie Heinekenplein** until it was demolished in 1988, yet this cafe-ringed, 1993-built semicircular 'square' is named for the founder's niece, painter Marie Heineken (1844–1930), famed for her still-life flowers.

8 Famous Selfies

On Frans Halsstraat, **Wake Me Up When I'm Famous**, by Jurriaan and Rinus van Hall, is a 2013 street-art mural with the words stencilled in white on a black background and selfie-favourite bench in front.

EXPERIENCES

Browse the Albert Cuypmarkt
MARKET

MAP: ① P118 B1

A hive of activity, the **Albert Cuypmarkt** *(albertcuyp-markt. amsterdam)* has been the heart and soul of De Pijp since it was established in 1905. Named for landscape painter Albert Cuyp (1620–91), this unmissable street market, stretching for 700m along Albert Cuypstraat between Ferdinand Bolstraat to its west and Van Woustraat to its east, is the biggest and best known in the Netherlands. From 9.30am to 5pm Monday to Saturday, some 260 stalls sell everything from fresh produce, ready-to-eat treats and bouquets of flowers to fabrics, clothing, cosmetics and much more.

Picnic in Sarphatipark
PARK

De Pijp's favourite hangout on sunny days is the **Sarphatipark** (MAP: ② P118 B2). Created in 1885, this English-style urban oasis takes in 4.5 hectares of ponds, meadows and wooded fringes. At its centre is the 1886 temple-style **Sarphati Memorial**, with a fountain, gargoyles and a bust of doctor, businessman and urban innovator Samuel Sarphati (1813–66), for whom the park is named.

The gently sloping lawns here are idyllic for picnics (pick up provisions at the Albert Cuypmarkt, and chilled craft brews at **Bier Baum**; MAP: ③ P118 B2). There's a playground for littlies and a nature play area for older kids.

Sample De Pijp Bites
TOUR

Dive into De Pijp's global food scene on a small-group insiders' tours (maximum eight people) with **Hungry Birds** *(hungry birds.nl; short flight/original tour €79/110)*. Guides take you 'off the eaten track' to chow on Dutch and world specialities, visiting local hotspots from street vendors to family-run premises on 2½- to three-hour 'short flight' tours or 4½-hour original tours that have been running in De Pijp for over a decade. Prices include all food; the meet-up location is given after you make reservations. It also runs tours in Amsterdam's multicultural **Oost** (p133).

See Emerging Acts
ENTERTAINMENT

With a capacity of just 150, **Cinetol** (MAP: ④ P118 H1; *cinetol.nl*) is an intimate place to catch established and emerging local acts across all genres: indie, folk, jazz, R&B, soul, rock, pop, punk, post-punk, garage, psychedelic, hip-hop, Afrobeat, EDM... Around 250 concerts take place each year; it also hosts exhibitions, screenings and album launches. Its on-site Tolbar cafe opens out onto a sunny terrace.

'Cultural clubhouse' **CC Amstel** (MAP: ⑤ P118 H1; *ccamstel.nl*) presents performing arts events from circus to dance and visual theatre and art exhibitions.

Go to the Movies
CINEMA

MAP: **6** P118 **B2**

Opened in 1921, art-deco cinema **Rialto** *(rialtofilm.nl)* shows eclectic arthouse fare from around the world (many in English or with English subtitles). Buy tickets online or at the box office.

Study Up on Amsterdam School Architecture
MUSEUM, TOURS

MAP: **7** P118 **C3**

Designed by two of the Amsterdam School's founding members, Piet Kramer and Michel de Klerk, social housing complex De Dageraad (meaning 'the dawn') was a game-changer when it was completed in 1922. The architects devised buildings that were not only functional but also artistic, as evident in the wave-like brick facades' rounded edges, flowing balconies, integrated sculptures and wrought-ironwork.

Plans of De Pijp, floor plans, stained glass, sculptures and photos are displayed at its **Museum De Dageraad** *(hetschip.nl; museum adult/child €16.50/5, architectural walks €13.50)*, accessed from Burgemeester Tellegenstraat. Museum tickets include a tour of the complex (the 3.30pm tour is in English). Check the agenda for two-hour walking tours of Amsterdam School architecture in the surrounding area.

The organisation also runs the Museum Het Schip in the 1921 Amsterdam School housing complex in Amsterdam West.

Admire Amsterdam's Century-Old Olympic Stadium
STADIUM

Built for the 1928 Olympic Games, the elegant **Olympisch Stadion Amsterdam** (MAP: **8** P118 **D3**; *olympischstadion.nl; tour from €12.50*) is a triumph of Amsterdam School architecture, designed by Jan Wils, a protégé of HP Berlage.

AMSTERDAM'S PLAN ZUID

At the turn of the 20th century, HP (Hendrik Petrus) Berlage was tasked with urbanising Amsterdam's then-undeveloped south. In line with the city's 1901 housing act to improve workers' housing supply, affordability and standards, and avoid slums, Berlage's 1915 Plan Zuid ('South Plan') of wide streets, greenery-filled courtyards and decorative bridges was brought to life by architects from the expressionist Amsterdam School. Boosted by Amsterdam's 1928 Olympic Games, the Amsterdam School's design philosophy spanned housing blocks with brick sculptures with curved corners, odd windows and rocket-shaped towers to streetlights, bridges, rubbish bins and electricity substations.

It has a soaring tower from which the Olympic flame burned for the first time during competition, and has been restored to again host track-and-field events. Concerts, festivals and other events also take place here; on King's Day, it hosts massive music festival **Kingsland** *(kingslandfestival.nl)*. Arrange guided one-hour tours (minimum of five people) in advance.

On Saturdays, the small, friendly neighbourhood market **Stadionpleinmarkt** (MAP: **9** P118 D3; *facebook.com/Stadionpleinmarkt*) sets up on Stadionplein.

Explore the Amstelpark PARK

Rose and rhododendron gardens, a glasshouse and orangery grace the **Amstelpark** (MAP: **10** P118 G4; *amstelpark.info*), open 7am to 10pm April to September, until 6pm October to March, created for the 1972 flower show Floriade. At its southern edge near 1636 polder-drainage windmill **De Riekermolen** (MAP: **11** P118 G5) is a statue of Rembrandt sketching it. Amstelpark hosts the travelling artisan food, drink and design-filled **Pure Markt** *(puremarkt.nl)* on the second Sunday of the month from April to October. Festivals include epicurean highlights at **Bite of Amsterdam** *(biteof amsterdam.com)* in May; food-truck **Festival Trek** *(festival-trek. nl)* in July; and the **Amsterdam Wine Festival** *(amsterdamwine festival.nl)* in September.

Amstelpark activities include playgrounds, a city farm, yew-hedge maze, **mini golf** *(minigolf amstelpark.nl; from €9)*, and the delightful miniature **Amstel Trein** (Amstel Train; *amsteltrein. nl; €3.50)*, as well as rides for tots such as bumper boats at the **Speeltuin Amstelpark** *(speeltuin -amstelpark.nl; 1/10 tokens €1.30/12)*; check individual seasonal opening times online.

Marvel at the World's Largest Floriculture Marketplace FACTORY
MAP: **12** P118 A6

Southwest of Amsterdamse Bos near Schiphol Airport in Aalsmeer, international growers' cooperative **Royal FloraHolland** (*royalflora holland.com; adult/child €12/9.50)* is a massive facility the size of 250 football fields, where millions of colourful blooms on thousands of flower carts are sorted by barcode and travel via monorail to be shipped across the world.

Self-guided tours that give you a bird's-eye view of the warehouse floor from an elevated walkway. It's open from 7am to 11am Monday, Tuesday, Wednesday and Friday, to 9am on Thursday; the earlier you arrive the more action you'll see. Take Connexxion bus 357 to Aalsmeer's Royal FloraHolland stop.

Create Content in an Instagram Fantasyland
PHOTOGRAPHY

MAP: 13 P118 G3

Across Europaplein from the RAI convention centre, **The Upside Down** *(the-upsidedown.com; adult/child from €20.95/14.95)* is a whirl of optical illusions (upside-down rooms, larger-than-life art) and vivid immersive experiences (a walk-in dress-up closet, silent disco and LED-light ball pit) over 25 photogenic spaces all designed to light up your IG or TikTok. Book a slot online, charge your phone and plan on around 90 minutes here.

Anticipate the Hartwig Museum
MUSEUM

Zuidas ('South Axis') is rapidly transforming beyond a business district. Massive infrastructure project Zuidasdok is seeing the A10 Zuid ring-road motorway widened and diverted underground, and train station **Amsterdam Zuid** becoming a major transport hub, with international rail services. Amsterdam will gain a major contemporary art museum here when the **Hartwig Museum** (MAP: 14 P118 E3; *hartwigartfoundation.nl*) opens in 2028. Construction is underway on Parnassusweg 220. Established by the Hartwig Art Foundation, which presents works in locations citywide, the new museum's exhibitions will especially spotlight emerging young artists and create art in working artist studios.

BEST WATER ACTIVITIES

Boaty
MAP: 15 P118 G2

Electric boats carry up to six; rental includes a route map (no boat licence needed). Its Amstelkanaal jetty is an ideal launching pad before busy city-centre canals. *boaty.nl*

SUP Tropisch
MAP: 16 P118 G2

By the Amstelkanaal, SUP Tropisch hires SUPs, has route options for all levels and organises magical nighttime trips under the stars. *suptropisch.nl*

SUP Rental Amsterdam
MAP: 17 P118 H2

Rent stable Red Paddle SUPs (with instruction for beginners) by the Berlagebrug on the Amstel. *amsterdamboothuur.nl*

SUP SUP CLUB
MAP: 18 P118 H3

Book online to open SUP 2 GO lockers in multiple locations including the Amstel Boathouse. *supsupclub.com*

Ahead of its opening, temporary public space **Hartwig Proxy** (MAP: 19 P118 E3), nearby at Parnassusweg 213, provides a preview of what's in store, acting as a 'testing ground' for the upcoming museum and an artistic gathering space.

See p118 for map of locations

Best Places for...

€ Budget €€ Midrange €€€ Top End

Eating

Brunch

Bakers & Roasters €€
 20 A1

Brazilian–Kiwi favourite for banana-nut-bread French toast, Navajo eggs, smoked-salmon stacks and passionfruit caipirinhas. *8.30am-3pm Mon-Fri, to 4pm Sat & Sun*

Little Collins €€
21 C1

Creative dishes include oat-milk panna cotta with rhubarb or poached eggs with smoked labneh and dukka, plus fermented-chilli Bloody Marys. Walk-ins only. *9am-4pm*

Vinnies €€
22 G2

Fabulous all-day brunch dishes span blueberry spelt pancakes and grain-free coconut granola to spicy shakshuka, and mimosas. *7.30am-5pm Mon-Fri, 9am-5pm Sat & Sun*

Miri Mary €€
23 B2

Weekend brunch with an Indian twist like butter chicken eggs Benny or masala omelettes. *5.30-10pm Mon-Thu, 10.30am-3pm & 5.30-10pm Fri-Sun*

Cafe Dishes

SLA €
 24 B2

Stylish salad bar (sit-down or take away) with a zero-waste, organic kitchen for 'create-your-own' salads, wraps, bowls, smoothies, juices and kombucha. *11.30am-9pm*

De Dakduif €
25 B1

Filled baguettes, soups, savoury pies and De Pijp's best cinnamon-crusted apple pie. *10am-6pm Mon-Wed, 10am-midnight Thu & Fri, 9am-midnight Sat, 11am-6pm Sun*

Café My Place €
26 B2

Plant-filled cafe with a sunny terrace and great open-faced sandwiches, that morphs into an evening cocktail bar with DJs. *11am-8pm Wed, Thu & Sun, to 1am Fri & Sat*

Contemporary Dining

Bisous €€€
27 A2

French/Zeeland cuisine (eg *sole meunière*) in a dramatic interior that feels like dining inside a giant Piet Mondrian painting. *5.30-10pm Mon-Wed, noon-10pm Thu-Sat*

Graham's Kitchen €€€
28 C1

Chef Graham Mee's intricate menus (no à la carte) feature dishes like waffles with black-pearl caviar or amberjack with tofu brûlée. *6-10.30pm Tue-Sat*

Het Bosch €€€
29 C4

On the banks of the Nieuwe Meer with a waterside terrace, celebrating local vegetables and line-caught and hand-harvested seafood. *noon-3pm & 6-9pm Mon-Fri, 6-9pm Sat*

Tapas-Style Dining

Kaasbar €€
 30 A1

Classy space with a conveyor belt of 20+ cloche-covered Dutch cheeses winding by diners

EXPLORE

DE PIJP & ZUID

to pair with 40+ by-the-glass wines. *5-11pm Mon-Thu, 1pm-1am Fri-Sun*

Juno
31 **A1**
Open-flame-grilled dishes complement over 40 natural wines in the dark-timber interior or under the fairy-light-strung trees outside. *5pm-midnight Tue-Fri, 1pm-midnight Sat & Sun*

Sol El Luna
32 **A2**
Tapas and cocktail bar with sharing dishes like *pimientos de padrón*, grilled octopus and *jamón ibérico*. *5-11pm Tue-Fri, noon-11pm Sat & Sun*

Drinking

Bars

Bar Mokum
33 **A1**
Ode to Mokum (Amsterdam's nickname), mixing cocktails made with local spirits and liqueurs, with décor re-creating its streetscapes. *5pm-1am Mon-Thu, to 2am Fri & Sat*

Brouwerij Troost
34 **A3**
Watch beer being brewed in stainless-steel vats at this original location of the organic craft brewery. *4pm-1am Mon-Thu, 4pm-2am Fri, noon-2am Sat, noon-11pm Sun*

Café Sarphaat
35 **C2**
Perennial local favourite opposite Sarphatipark with a lovely old bar and outdoor terrace that's heated in chilly weather. *9am-1am Sun-Thu, to 3am Fri & Sat*

Barça
36 **B1**
On bar-filled Marie Heinekenplein, with a 'Barcelona in Amsterdam' theme, Spanish wines and sparkling cava. *noon-midnight Sun-Thu, to 1am Wed & Thu, to 3am Fri & Sat*

Shopping

Fashion & Accessories

Elcie
37 **B1**
Elsbeth Schiphorst makes dresses, tops, jackets and leggings from leftover fabrics at her De Pijp studio. *noon-6pm Wed-Sun*

De Kleine Parade
38 **B1**
A selection of adorable kids' and babies' clothing, shoes, accessories and toys, and children's hair salon. *9.30am-2pm Mon, 9.30am-5pm Tue-Sat, 11am-5pm Sun*

Mercer
39 **A1**
Sustainable streetwear and vegan sneakers made from pineapple leather, grapes, cacti or plastic ocean waste. *1-6pm Mon, 10am-6pm Tue-Sat, noon-5pm Sun*

Love Stories Archive
40 **B1**
Samples, stock sales and discounted lingerie and swimwear by Dutch designer Marloes Hoedeman. *noon-6pm*

Cycling Gear

Maats
41 **C2**
Cycling clothing and accessories; also organises city and countryside bike rides. *maats.cc, 10am-6pm Tue-Sat, noon-5pm Sun*

Gifts & Souvenirs

De Winkel van Nijntje
42 **G2**
Dedicated Miffy (Nijntje in Dutch) emporium filled with cuddly toys, prints, lamps, clothing, posters, magnets, notebooks and more. *11.30am-6pm Mon, 10am-6pm Tue-Sat, noon-6pm Sun*

for eating,
drinking and
shopping
listings

Explore

Oosterpark & East of the Amstel

*Researched by
Barbara Woolsey &
Catherine Le Nevez*

Oost (East) is one of Amsterdam's most culturally diverse neighbourhoods. It grew up in the 19th century, a heritage recalled in its grand buildings, wide boulevards and beautiful English-style Oosterpark, where in 2023, King Willem-Alexander formally apologised for the Netherlands' involvement in slavery – the Keti Koti ('broken chains') commemoration takes place here on 1 July every year. Lush expanses and wetlands further east date from when this area was a country retreat. Today's Oost is one of Amsterdam's most rapidly gentrifying neighbourhoods. Scout out trendy set-menu restaurants and bars – from rooftop bars with stupendous views to a park-hidden *jenever* (Dutch gin) distillery.

Getting Around

Tram

From Centraal Station, tram 14 skirts Oosterpark's northern edge. Trams 1 and 3 run past Oosterpark on their east–west routes across the city. Tram 19 runs north–south through the neighbourhood's centre.

Metro

Lines 51, 53 and 54 run south from Centraal Station along the neighbourhood's western border.

Cycling

This spread-out area and its sprawling parks are especially suited to exploring by bike; there's a 2km loop around Oosterpark and a 5km loop in Park Frankendael.

THE BEST

MUSEUM
Wereldmuseum
Amsterdam (p136)

PARK
Oosterpark (p140)

DISTILLERY
Distilleerderij 't Nieuwe
Diep (p139)

GREENHOUSE RESTAURANT
De Kas (p141)

ROOFTOP BAR
Canvas (p141)

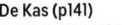

De Kas (p141)
RINZE VEGELIEN, VIA DE KAS

PLANTAGE

Artis Zoo

Plantage Middenlaan

Plantage Muidergracht

Plantage Muidergracht

Rioletersstr

Nieuwe Achtergr

Spinozastr

Singelgracht

Sajetplein

Mauritskade

Alexanderplein

Sarphati...

Alexanderkade

Singelgracht

Mauritskade

🏛 **Wereldmuseum Amsterdam**

17

19 1e Van Swindenstr

14 2e Van Swindenstr

1 Oosterpark

Linnaeusstr

OOSTERPARKBUURT

Ruyschstr

Ruyschstraat

Campenstr

3e Oosterparkstr

2e Oosterparkstr

3e Oosterparkstr

12

Poputterenweg

Elsenweg

Tugelaweg

Wibautstr

M Wibautstraat

15

Pretoriusstr

Schalk Burgerstr

Transvaalkade

Ringvaart

Ringdijk

Amstel

Amsteldijk

Weesperzijde

8

Stephensonstr

Nobelweg

16

Ringdijkstr

TRANSVAALBUURT

4

0   600 m
0   0.3 miles

E   F   G   H

Zeeburgerdijk

DAPPERBUURT

1

Borneostr

Studio K   6

Bankastr

Molukkenstr

Madurastr   13

10

Javastr   9

Javastr

Calabstraat

Sumatrastr

18

Ballistr

1e Atjehstr

1e Atjehstr

INDISCHE BUURT

2

Pontanusstr

2e Atjehstr

Dapperstr

21

Dapperplein

Insulindeweg

Reinwardtstr

Insulindeweg

Muiderpoort

3

Molukkenstr

Valentijnkade

Polderweg

Polderweg

Ringvaart

Waldenlaan

Q-Factory   5

Linnaeuskade

4

Archimedesweg

Hogeweg

Copernicusstr

20

Middenweg

Linnaeusparkweg

5

Galileiplantsoe

Kamerlingh Onneslaan

11

Huize Frankendael

3

Hugo de Vrieslaan

2

Park Frankendael

Middenweg

7

For more see

Top Experiences ⭐ p136
Experiences ⭐ p140
Eating ✷ p141
Drinking 🅟 p141
Shopping 🅟 p141

6

Sportpark Voorland

135

E   F   G   H

★ TOP EXPERIENCE

Wereldmuseum Amsterdam

The Dutch slave trade, understanding cultural appropriation, and returning stolen artefacts to Indonesia – at the Wereldmuseum Amsterdam, themes around race, ethnicity and identity are explored from multiple perspectives. Such exhibits are part of the ethnographic museum's greater vision to examine and undo colonial practices of its past.

MAP P134 **C2**

PLANNING TIP
Allow several hours to see everything. Excellent temporary exhibitions (included in admission) dive deeper into topics such as restitution or martial arts around the world.

Scan this QR code for full opening details and to book tickets.

An Existential Reckoning

In 2023, the Tropenmuseum (Royal Tropics Museum), one of Europe's leading ethnographic museums, changed its name – a symbolic break from over 150 years of tradition.

Today, the Wereldmuseum (World Museum) is addressing how its colonial past might still be shaping modern institutional practices, from rethinking how objects are displayed to whether they should be repatriated, and, overall, how history can become more inclusive. Deeply immersive, modern multimedia exhibitions are staged within the museum's grand neo-Renaissance architecture.

Koloniaal Museum

The Wereldmuseum's origins date back to 1871, when it was established as the Koloniaal Museum (Colonial Museum). Like many 19th-century European museums, the museum's collections grew out of colonial expansion and scientific research. A menagerie of possessions from colonised lands and peoples were displayed as symbols of Dutch colonial wealth.

After the Dutch colonial empire ended, the institution became the Royal Tropics Museum in 1950; shifting its focus to regions from Africa, to the Middle East and beyond.

WERELDMUSEUM

Exhibitions

Contrasting the atrium's stunning, old-world elegance with brightly lit, modern displays, the 2018-installed permanent exhibition **Things That Matter** explores universal cultural themes such as language, belief, climate and activism, honing in on questions such as 'When is culture yours?'

Spanning 1200 sq metres, the exhibition **Our Colonial Inheritance** is a profound, comprehensive inspection of Dutch colonial history. It delves into colonialism through wide-ranging access points. Most movingly, the **Digital Names Monument** is inscribed with the names of nearly 200,000 individuals who were enslaved during the colonial period in Suriname, Curaçao and Indonesia.

TAKE A BREAK
On the opposite side of the Linnaeusstraat boulevard to the museum, you'll find Surinamese cuisine at Roopram Roti (p141), and global street foods at the Dappermarkt (p141).

 **WALKING TOUR**

Amble Oosterpark & East of the Amstel

The richly multifaceted character of Amsterdam's east is revealed at every turn on this walk. Along the way, you'll check out soaring street-art murals, Oosterpark's pivotal national monument, a warehouse-set brewery, former bathhouse and an enchanting *jenever* distillery hidden in woodland in Flevopark, with a wilder, more rambling feel than Amsterdam's more central green spaces.

START	END	LENGTH
4850 (metro Wibautstraat)	Flevopark (tram 3 Flevopark)	5km; 2½hr

1 Caffeine Fix

Natural light floods the industrial-meets-mid-century interior of **4850** on Camperstraat. It's perfect for a daytime coffee and cardamom bun; by night it morphs into a wine bar.

2 Multi-Storey Street Art

One-off street-art festival 'If Walls Could Speak' (2019) left behind **soaring murals** on five apartment blocks on Platanenweg. They include pigeons featuring in *Floating Between Freedom* by Studio Giftig; a child's diary entry in *Little Wizard* by Herakut; and Amsterdam's city symbol of three St Andrew's crosses in *Het Wapen Verbroedert* by Kash & Chuck.

3 Momentous Monument

Slavery was abolished in the Dutch colonies of Suriname and the Netherlands Antilles in 1863, and Surinamese sculptor Erwin de Vries was commissioned in 2002 to create Oosterpark's bronze **Nationaal Slavernijmonument** (National Slavery Monument), which depicts both oppression and hope for the future.

4 Innovative Brews

Salted-caramel miso stout is among the inventive creations brewed on site at microbrewery **Brouwerij Poesiat & Kater**. Inside a converted brick warehouse, it has a spiral staircase leading to a mezzanine and 12m mural of the brewing process from fermentation to mashing and toasting. Outside is a huge waterside terrace for sampling its wares.

5 Orchestral Church

Designed by Jan Stuyt in 1925, Byzantine-inspired church Gerardus Majellakerk, with a 12-sided conical tower, is now the **NedPhO-Koepel**. Home to the Netherlands Philharmonic & Chamber Orchestra, it hosts free public rehearsals and concerts beneath the dome.

6 Neighbourhood Square

At Indische Buurt's heart, **Javaplein** has notable buildings including Hendrik Petrus Berlage's 1915 Berlageblokken housing complex, and Amsterdam's last public bathhouse, the 1942-built Badhuis, now a restaurant and performance space.

7 Fairy-Tale Flevopark Distillery

Appearing out of the woods like a Hansel and Gretel cottage, the quaint architecture and setting of this old pumping station, with a lakeside terrace next to an orchard, is enchanting. **Distilleerderij 't Nieuwe Diep** makes around 100 small-batch *jenevers*, herbal bitters, liqueurs and fruit distillates from organic ingredients according to old Dutch recipes.

EXPERIENCES

Unwind in the Oosterpark   PARK

MAP: **1** P134 **C3**

The **Oosterpark**'s lush greenery, with parakeets in the trees and herons stalking the large ponds, brings an almost tropical richness to this neighbourhood, despite being laid out in English style. Designed by Leonard Antonij Springer, it was established in 1891 as a pleasure park, and still retains an elegant feel. Tango sessions take place on alternate summer Sundays in the bandstand. Families will enjoy the playground (with a summer wading pool) on the park's north side.

Trace Park Frankendael's History   PARK

During the 17th century, Amsterdammers sought respite from the city. Drained in 1629, the polder area of Watergraafsmeer made way for country estates, farmlands and gardens. It was annexed in 1921 and absorbed into Amsterdam-Oost. **Park Frankendael**'s (MAP: **2** P134 **E6**) reedy areas' wildlife includes waterbirds, frogs and nesting storks.

Restored Louis XIV–style mansion **Huize Frankendael** (Frankendael House; MAP: **3** P134 **F6**; *huizefrankendael.nl; free*) is Amsterdam's last remaining country estate; within its coach house is elegant restaurant **Merkelbach** (*restaurantmerkelbach.nl*). Huize Frankendael opens to the public on the last Sunday of every month, when the artisan **Pure Markt** also sets up.

Tour AFC Ajax's Home Turf   STADIUM

MAP: **4** P134 **B6**

The Netherlands' most famous football team, AFC Ajax, plays its home games at 1996-opened 68,000-capacity **Johan Cruijff ArenA**. Match tickets are sold on its website (*johancruijffarena.nl; from €80*).

Highlights of self-guided tours (*adult/child €27.50/19.25*) include emerging from the 'Players Tunnel' to the edge of the pitch and commemorative Delftware porcelain in the memorabilia-packed Ajax Gallery of Fame.

BEST ENTERTAINMENT

Q-Factory

MAP: **5** P134 **E3**

Rock, metal, soul, funk, electronica and dance events raise the roof at Europe's biggest music-making centre, with on-site recording studios. *q-factory-amsterdam.nl*

Studio K

MAP: **6** P134 **F1**

Arts centre with cinema halls, a nightclub, a stage for bands and theatre. *studio-k.nu*

Kwaku

MAP: **7** P134 **G6**

Live music and dance performances feature at this massive food-and-football fair celebrating Surinamese culture on summer weekends. *kwakufestival.nl*

Best Places for...

€ Budget €€ Midrange €€€ Top End

See p134 for map of locations

Eating

Locavore Dining

Vergulden Eenhoorn €€
 C6

Seasonal dining in a restored 1702-built farmhouse with leather sofas, indoor fireplace and summer terrace. *10am-11pm*

Wilde Zwijnen €€ €
9 G2

Rustic-industrial space using regional, sustainable produce. *6-10pm Mon, Tue & Thu-Sat, noon-10pm Sun*

La Douzaine €€
10 G1

Oysters and seafood with bubbles and wine at outdoor barrel-tables on Javastraat. *3-9.30pm Wed & Thu, noon-10.30pm Fri & Sat, noon-8pm Sun*

De Kas €€€ €
 E5

Michelin-starred multi-course dining, growing most of its own produce in 1926 greenhouses. *noon-1.45pm & 6-9pm Mon-Sat*

Picnic Fare & Quick Eats

Erik's Delicatessen €
 C4

Cheeses, charcuterie, fresh bread, tapenades, olives, salads and canned and bottled preserves, vinegars and oils. *8am-6pm Mon-Sat, 9am-6pm Sun*

Gallizia €
 F1

Laden daytime Italian deli adjoining a cosy evening bar-resto for an antipasti adventure. *hours vary*

Roopram Roti €
14 D2

Canteen-style Surinamese cafe for flaky lamb roti and *barra* (lentil doughnut) – don't forget the fiery hot sauce. *2-9pm Tue-Sun*

Drinking

Rooftop Bars

Canvas
15 A5

Weekend DJs, summer events like cinema screenings, and Sunday access to hot tubs. *7am-1am Mon-Fri, 8am-3am Sat, to 1am Sun*

Dakterras GAPP
16 C6

Creative cocktails amongst an aromatic herb garden. *noon-10pm Fri & Sat, 9am-5pm Sun*

Fitz's on the Roof
17 C2

Umbrella-shaded, 4th-floor rooftop terrace overlooking Oosterpark. *5pm-midnight Sun-Thu, 4pm-1am Fri & Sat*

Neighbourhood Bars

Bar Basquiat
18 F2

Local beers, well-made cocktails and excellent Indonesian street food. *11am-1am Mon-Thu, to 2am Fri & Sat, to 11pm Sun*

De Biertuin
19 D2

Covered terrace and heaters, plus a lengthy beer list. *3pm-1am Mon-Thu, to 2am Fri, noon-2am Sat, to 1am Sun*

Cafe Mojo
20 E4

Lovely open-fronted bar right by the canal with a superb terrace. *noon-midnight Mon-Wed, to 1am Thu, to 3am Fri, to 2am Sat, 11am-11pm Sun*

Shopping

Dappermarkt
21 E2

Around 250 stalls sell food (dried apricots, olives, fish, Turkish kebabs) and goods (costume jewellery, clothes, toys and electronics). *10am-5pm Mon-Sat*

See p156
for eating,
drinking and
shopping
listings

Explore

Researched by
Mark Elliott

Nieuwmarkt, Plantage & the Eastern Islands

Immediately east of the centre, buzzing Nieuwmarkt is sewn through with rich seams of history. Here you'll find the Museum Rembrandthuis – the Old Master's home and studio, where he lived and painted during his most successful years – as well as insightful museums housed in centuries-old synagogues in the old Jewish quarter. Nearby, entering the leafy Plantage takes it down a gear, with the sprawling zoo and botanical gardens. The greenery of the Plantage segues into the Eastern Islands, where there's a completely different atmosphere of maritime history combined with ex-warehouses transformed into contemporary bars along with flagship modern Dutch architecture.

Getting Around

🚲 Walking & Cycling
Walking is the best way to cover the western half of this neighbourhood; you'll need a bike or public transport to the east.

🚊 Tram & Bus
IJburg-bound tram 26 from Centraal follows the IJ, intersecting with tram 7 at Rietlandpark. Tram 14 goes via Waterlooplein and Plantage. Buses 22 and 43 serve Eastern Islands areas.

Ⓜ Metro
Metro lines 51, 53 and 54 connect Centraal Station via Nieuwmarkt and Waterlooplein to Weesperplein.

★ THE BEST

ARTIST'S HOME
Museum Rembrandthuis (p146)

MARITIME MUSEUM
Het Scheepvaartmuseum (p150)

SCIENCE EXPERIMENTS
NEMO (p150)

CONCERT HALL
Muziekgebouw aan 't IJ (p155)

ZOO
Artis (p150)

Het Scheepvaartmuseum (p150)
JOYFULL/SHUTTERSTOCK

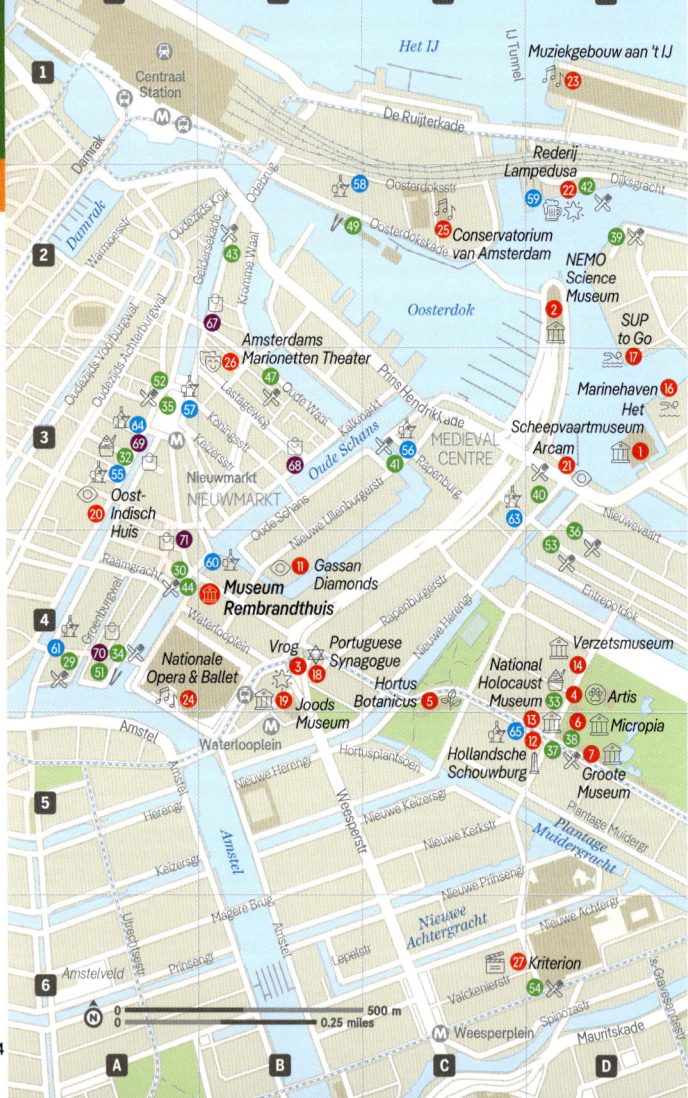

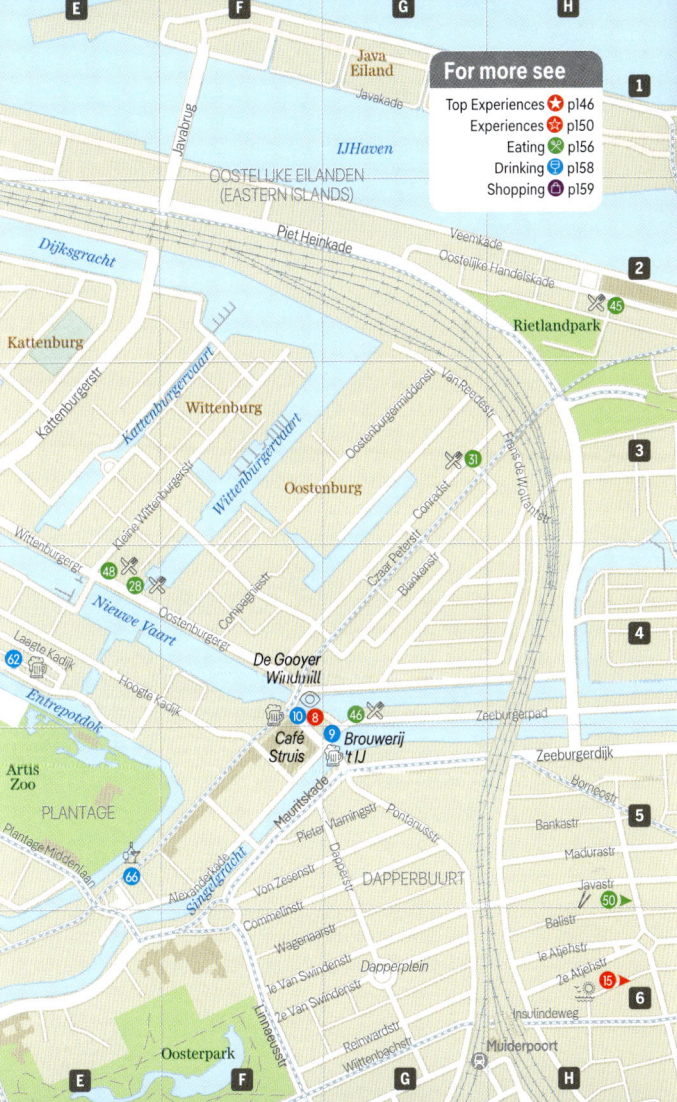

E | F | G | H

1

Java Eiland

Javakade

IJHaven

For more see

Top Experiences ⭐ p146
Experiences ⭐ p150
Eating 🍴 p156
Drinking 🍷 p158
Shopping 🛍 p159

Javabrug

OOSTELIJKE EILANDEN
(EASTERN ISLANDS)

Dijksgracht

Piet Heinkade

Veemkade

Oostelijke Handelskade

2

Kattenburg

Kattenburgerstr

Kattenburgervaart

Wittenburg

Wittenburgervaart

Oostenburg

Oostenburgermiddenstr

Van Reigersbos

Rietlandpark

🍴 45

Prins de Wolienstr

3

Kleine Wittenburgerstr

Wittenburgerstr

Compagniestr

Oostenburgerstr

Czaar Peterstr

Blankenstr

🌳 31

48

28

Nieuwe Vaart

Oostenburgergr

4

Laagte Kadijk

62

Hoogte Kadijk

De Gooyer Windmill

🍺 10 8

🌳 46

Zeeburgerpad

5

Entrepotdok

Café Struis

9 Brouwerij 't IJ

Zeeburgerdijk

Bornest

Artis Zoo

PLANTAGE

Mauritskade

Pieter Vlamingstr

Pontanusstr

Zeeburgerstr

Bankastr

Madurastr

Plantage Middenlaan

66

Alexanderkade

Singelgracht

Von Zesenstr

Dappelstr

DAPPERBUURT

Dapperplein

Javastr

Balistr

🌳 50

6

Commelinstr

Wagenaarstr

1e Van Swindenstr

1e Atjehstr

2e Atjehstr

🍴 15

Linnaeusstr

1e Van Swindenstr

Reinwardtstr

Wittenbachstr

Insulindeweg

Oosterpark

Muiderpoort

E | F | G | H

145

⭐ **TOP EXPERIENCE**

Museum Rembrandthuis

Explore the 1606 canal house of one of the Netherlands' greatest artistic geniuses, Rembrandt van Rijn, which he bought in 1639, helped by his wealthy wife, Saskia van Uylenburgh. Interiors are meticulously reconstructions based on a detailed inventory made in 1656 when bankruptcy forced Rembrandt to sell it.

MAP P144 **B4**

PLANNING TIP
Pre-book timeslot entry; at quiet times (typically midweek afternoons), walk-ins are usually possible. Live demonstrations of pigment making or etching are included on alternate days (10.30am-noon & 12.30-3pm).

Scan this QR code for full opening hours and information on booking.

Kitchen & Courtyard

Collect your audio guide from the modern annexe then start a visit on the lower level in the kitchen. Most of the pots and crockery are from other sources but a glass box displays a few originals including tobacco pipes later discovered in an archaeological excavation. The small open courtyard, home to a wooden toilet cubicle, is thought to be where Rembrandt painted *The Night Watch* (the studio wouldn't have been big enough).

Voorhuys & Sijdelcaemer

The high-ceilinged *voorhuys* (hall) doubled as a gallery and sales room showing work to potential purchasers. Paintings displayed here now are mostly by artists who inspired Rembrandt's early work, notably including Pieter Lastman (1583–1633).

Clients interested in commissioning work would be ushered through into the *sijdelcaemer* (antechamber) to discuss terms over a glass of wine. It now displays paintings by Rembrandt's apprentice-students.

Etchings

Partway up the narrow staircase, a small side-room displays just a handful of Rembrandt's etchings from the museum's collection (including 285 of 310 known designs). Lifting the protective leather flaps reveals mostly tiny originals. Other displays show how etchings look on different papers and a sniff box to experience the perfume of the ink.

AAD HOOGENDOORN, VIA MUSEUM REMBRANDTHUIS

Studio & Cabinet

Continue up the narrow staircase to the master's studio, ideally light-filled thanks to four north-facing windows. Every second day there are a fascinating demonstrations here on how Rembrandt selected and ground pigments with linseed oil to make paints. Across the landing is Rembrandt's 'Cabinet', a room crammed with curiosities similar to those he collected: giant clamshells, an Amazonian macaw-feather headdress, busts of Roman philosophers, stuffed alligators and much more – all used at times as subjects for sketches.

Student & Etching Studios

The next floor up houses the etching studio with demonstrations; otherwise, watch a video version on the large screen horizontal screen-table. Across the landing is the studio where apprentices worked in three separate booths. Exit via two large rooms of temporary exhibitions.

QUICK BREAK
Have lunch at light-filled cafe **TisFris** (p156), only a few doors away. Or linger over a canal-side drink and snack at 17th-century **De Sluyswacht** (p158), right on the waterfront.

🚶 WALKING TOUR

Navigate Nieuwmarkt & Plantage

Nieuwmarkt's action-packed plaza and Plantage's garden-district greenery make for lively and lovely strolling. Distinctive cafes are the bonus here: they pop up in rustic shipping warehouses, 17th-century lock-keepers' quarters, the turreted city gate and just about everywhere in between. A flea market adds to the daily buzz. Allow time to stop off along the way.

START	END	LENGTH
De Druif (Centraal Station)	Scheepvaarthuis (Centraal Station)	3.5km; 2hr

❶ History-Steeped Café

In a building dating from 1566, **De Druif** (*instagram.com/cafe_de_druif*), meaning 'the Grape', gained its first liquor licence in 1631, and acted as an embarkation *café* (pub), where sailors came to register for work on Dutch East India Company (VOC) ships. Its time as a former distillery is evident in its wooden spirit barrels behind the bar.

❷ Dockside at Entrepotdok

The VOC, which grew rich on sea trade in the 17th century, owned **Entrepotdok**, a 500m row of warehouses that was the largest storage depot in Europe at the time. It's now packed with offices, apartments and dockside cafes perfect for lazing away a few hours at the water's edge, looking across to the Artis Zoo (p150).

❸ Wertheimpark's Memorial

Opposite the Hortus Botanicus (p151), **Wertheimpark** is a willow-shaded spot brilliant for relaxing by the Nieuwe Herengracht – it's a great place to escape the crowds for a while. On the park's northeast side, locals often place flowers at the **Auschwitz Memorial**, a panel of broken mirrors installed in the ground that reflects the sky.

❹ Flea Market Finds

Covering the square once known as Vlooienburg (Flea Town) daily except Sunday, the **Waterlooplein Flea Market** (*waterlooplein. amsterdam*) draws sharp-eyed customers seeking everything from antique knick-knacks to designer knock-offs and cheap bicycle locks in among some tourist tat. The street market started in 1880, when Jewish traders living in the neighbourhood started selling their wares here.

❺ Castle-Like Gate

The Waag was built as a gate in the city walls in 1488. In 1601, the walls were demolished as the city expanded and the building was turned into Amsterdam's main weigh house – which back then was a spot for public executions. A bar-restaurant occupies it today. The masons' guild was based in the tower facing the Zeedijk; note the superfine brickwork. Out front, Nieuwmarkt hosts a variety of events, including a Saturday farmers market.

❻ Amsterdam School Architecture

Finish your walk with a nose around the supreme example of the Amsterdam School, **Scheepvaarthuis** (Shipping House; *amrathamsterdam.com*), with its nautical motifs, masterly stained glass and beautiful art-deco cafe. It's now open to guests as the **Grand Hotel Amrath**, but staff are more than happy for tourists to look around.

EXPERIENCES

Board a Replica Galleon

MUSEUM

MAP: **1** P144 **D3**

A full-scale replica of the 700-tonne galleon *Amsterdam* is the highlight of a visit to **Het Scheepvaartmuseum** (National Maritime Museum; *hetscheepvaartmuseum.com; adult/student/under-13 €18.50/8.50/free*). The original, one of the VOC's largest tall-mast ships, was wrecked by storms during its maiden voyage to east Asia. The tiny bunks, swinging hammocks, low beams and dangerous overhead ropes hint at how difficult life was for sailors. In the hold, you can try lifting heavy box-crates by pulley. In the prow, a 180-degree multi-screen projection takes you downriver on a virtual journey into the 18th-century port of Amsterdam. Signboards reflect the realities that the VOC's trade was, by today's standards, worse than theft.

Inside the main museum, the powerful exhibition *Shadows on the Atlantic* examines colonial reverberations. Other rooms display historic ship figureheads, navigational instruments and priceless naval charts.

The imposing courtyard building is itself part of the attraction, a 1656 waterfront behemoth originally designed as a storehouse for the Admiralty of Amsterdam.

See Science at NEMO

MUSEUM

State-of-the-art **NEMO Science Museum** (MAP: **2** P144 **D2**; *nemo sciencemuseum.nl; admission €21.50*) is truly interactive with four floors of investigative mayhem that kids of all ages will enjoy. Experiment with lifting yourself up via a pulley, making bubbles, building structures such as dams and test the forces acting on them, designing your own wind turbine, watching a chain-reaction display, riding a space-bike to the edge of the solar system, donning a lab coat for a hands-on chemistry session in the laboratory and testing your free will in psychology games. Almost everything is bilingual Dutch/English. You'll need several hours to see it all.

Impossible to miss, the green-copper building was designed by Italian architect Renzo Piano and is almost surrounded by water. The huge, sloping rooftop space, accessed via the museum or stairs in the southeastern corner, has some of the best views over Amsterdam.

Activities for kids around here also include **Vrog** (MAP: **3** P144 **B4**), with trick trampolining to parkour.

Meet Animals at Artis

ZOO

MAP: **4** P144 **D4**

Founded in 1838, **Artis** (*artis.nl; adult/child €30.50/29.50*) is one of Europe's oldest zoos. Its 14 leafy hectares are home to more than 750 animal species, from lions, jaguars, elephants and giraffes to sea lions, golden-cheeked gibbons, iguanas, flamingos and cassowaries. There's a reptile house, several aviaries and an aquarium. The butterfly pavilion has more than a thousand flittering creatures. You can journey through the solar system and Milky Way at the 324-seat planetarium (included in zoo admission).

While preserving much of its protected historic architecture, Artis has gone to enormous effort to update and enlarge its enclosures to ensure that its animal 'guests' remain healthy and happy. Since 2023, to help with their psychological wellbeing, lions have a wider variety of habitat including a high rocky perch from which they can see (if not hunt) zebras; elephants have a canal-fed bath-pond of 1.5 million litres; and the 1910 bird building incorporates a series of spacious inside-outside forest houses.

Take a Botany Lesson at the Hortus Botanicus   GARDEN

MAP: **5** P144 **C4**

A botanical garden since 1638, the Plantage's 1.2-hectare **Hortus Botanicus** (dehortus.nl; adult/child €13.50/7) bloomed as tropical seeds and plants were brought in by Dutch trading ships. From here, coffee, pineapple, cinnamon and palm-oil plants were distributed throughout the world. Its medicinal gardens provided the Netherlands' doctors with remedies. The gardens' 4000- plus species occupy wonderful structures including a 1911 palm house, butterfly house and three-climate glasshouse renewed as the world's first fully sustainable, climate-neutral greenhouse: carbon-neutral computer technology tweaks humidity and temperatures

are balanced using several 'waste' heat sources. The 1875 orangery shelters a lovely cafe.

Look Beyond the Visible   MUSEUM

MAP: **6** P144 **D5**

Micropia (artis.nl/en/artis -micropia; adult/student/under-13 €17.50/8.75/free) focuses on lifeforms too small to see with the naked eye. Peer through microscopes and discover unsettling facts about how many living organisms there are around us every day. Dare to take a body scan and become acquainted with your own microorganisms; learn the unromantic side of locking lips via the kiss-o-meter; and appreciate the beauty of viruses from Ebola to HIV – at least when they're glass models.

Combined tickets are available with nearby attractions Artis Zoo and Groote Museum.

Ask the Big Questions   MUSEUM

MAP: **7** P144 **D5**

What is the meaning of life? Forty-two, per The Hitchhikers' Guide to the Galaxy? Reproduction? The highly enjoyable **Groote Museum** (artis.nl/en/artis-groote-museum; adult/student/under-18 €17.50/10/ free) is called groote (big) because it attempts to ask such questions, particularly through examining natural cycles, connections across species and how our senses affect our perception and feelings. You can walk through a scent tunnel, drag yourself back through human evolution by tugging an umbilical cord, try to beat a chimp at a number memory game, and so much more.

Sip Beer by a Windmill
BREWERY

If Amsterdam is going to be your only experience of the Netherlands and you really want to snap a photo of a windmill, a great option is to jump on tram 7 to **De Gooyer Windmill** (MAP: **8** P144 **F4**). Built in 1725 but moved here in 1814, it's Amsterdam's largest, complete with creaking sails and pretty night-time lighting. You can't go inside as it's now a private house but the attached former bathhouse is now one of Amsterdam's leading microbreweries, **Brouwerij 't IJ** (MAP: **9** P144 **G5**; *brouwerijhetij.nl/ proeflokaal-de-molen; 2-10pm*). It offers a dozen excellent draft beers, such as Nijpa, a fruity full-flavoured IPA, and Zatte, a Belgian style triple, to savour on the plane-tree-shaded terrace. Once the main tasting room closes, head to adjacent co-owned **Café Struis** (MAP: **10** P144 **F4**).

Watch Gem-Grinders Work
FACTORY

MAP: **11** P144 **B4**

Gassan Diamonds (*gassan.com/ en/tours/diamond-experience-tour*) offers a fascinating and totally free opportunity to see diamond cutters in action. You can reserve an arrival slot online but it's often possible to join a tour at short notice by simply showing up at the restored 1879 factory building. The visit includes an engaging museum section about the industry, the family company's history and the various gem-cutting possibilities: Gassan 121 is their own trademarked style.

Visitors are then ushered to sit around a viewing table and guess the value of real diamonds while perusing Gassan jewellery. There's no pressure to buy and you can simply wander off and have a free coffee in the factory's former boiler-house as you exit. Plan for at least 40 minutes.

JEWISH AMSTERDAM IN WWII

Nieuwmarkt's Jewish quarter evolved from the 16th century and by Napoleonic times, Amsterdam was Europe's largest Jewish centre. During French rule, guilds that prohibited Jews and remaining restrictions were abolished, and Amsterdam's Jewish community thrived in the 19th and early 20th centuries. The Nazis' devastation of Amsterdam's Jewish community was near-total: of a pre-war population of some 90,000 Jews (13% of the city's population), only 5500, scarcely one in 16 people, survived. Amsterdammers resisted: the city's motto, *Heldhaftig, Vastberaden, Barmhartig* (Valiant, Steadfast, Compassionate), presented by Queen Wilhelmina in 1947, commemorates citizens' protests against the WWII persecution of Jews.

Honour the Legacy of Amsterdam's Jewish Community

MEMORIALS

From the road, the **Holland-sche Schouwburg** (MAP: 12 P144 D5; *jck.nl/en/location/hollandsche -schouwburg; free)* appears as it once was, an architecturally splendid 1892 theatre. However, behind the facade, the building is mostly a hollow shell: a powerful monument to the WWII deportations that virtually wiped out the Jewish community. An affecting 12-minute audio-visual tells the story of how, from 20 July 1942, the playhouse became a holding place from which around 46,000 Jews were eventually sent to prisons and death camps. After liberation, by the time the city could decide how to use the building, its rear section was in ruins. Ironically, the stark state of semi-collapse now serves to underline the sense of tragedy. Use your audio guide to listen to heart-rending personal tales of deportees as you walk towards the stark memorial obelisk.

Across the road, the **National Holocaust Museum** (MAP: 13 P144 D5; *adult/child €20/8)* is housed in a former school from which some Jewish children were spirited away to safety when passing trams masked the view of the guards.

Learn About the Dutch Resistance

MUSEUM

MAP: 14 P144 D4

What would you have done if you'd have lived in Amsterdam in WWII,

WATER SPORTS

Amsterdam's rapidly developing outer suburb of IJburg, reached via tram 26, is an urban water-sports getaway.

At wide, sandy artificial beach **Strand IJburg** (MAP: 15 P144 H6), container-housed **Surfcenter IJburg** *(surfcenterijburg.nl)* rents SUP boards, wingfoils and windsurfing gear. Nearby **King of Boardsports** *(kingofboardsports.com)* has wingfoil lessons and rentals.

By IJburg's marina, **Zeilschool IJburg** *(zeilschoolijburg.nl)* rents small skiffs and motorboats. Neighbouring **Amsterdam Watersports** *(amsterdamwatersports.com)* offers numerous activities including wakeboarding and flyboarding.

More central, near the Het Scheepvaartmuseum, **Marinehaven** (MAP: 16 P144 D3) has delineated swimming lanes. Across the inlet, **SUP to Go** (MAP: 17 P144 D3; *supsup club.com)* has automated lockers with SUP boards (prebook online).

a city suddenly occupied by Nazi Germans hell-bent on reorganising society to their ideology? It's a question you can't help but ask yourself at the sobering yet inspiring **Verzetsmuseum** (Dutch Resistance Museum; *verzetsmuseum.org; adult/student €14/7.50)*. Allow at least a couple of hours here to learn the background and then discover the ways in which people did react, whether by taking arms or more subtly by helping those in hiding, forging documents or contributing to underground newspapers, radios and general strikes. Nuanced personal stories illuminate people's complex predicaments rather than simply condemning those who failed to choose heroism.

An important side exhibit covers the WWII situation in the Dutch colonies, particularly the crushed early hopes amongst Indonesian independence activists.

The 'Junior' section, following four Dutch children, is a highlight of the whole museum.

See Saved Synagogues   SYNAGOGUES

Amsterdam's **Portuguese Synagogue** (aka Esnoga; MAP: **18** P144 **B4**; *jck.nl; adult/under-18/under-13 €22/10/7, €2 online discount*) was the largest in Europe when completed in 1675. The impressively tall prayer house is still active and retains many of its 17th-century features including sand-dusted floors to reduce noise, original pews with lockable seat-boxes and four towering stone pillars. Without electric light: candles are still lit in the vast chandeliers for services after dark, and during evening concerts (usually held one Thursday a month). To visit the 1616 **Ets Haim** *(jck.nl/ets-haim)*, the world's oldest still-active Jewish library, email ahead for an appointment, though a small sample is displayed.

Esnoga tickets include entrance to the **Joods Museum** (Jewish Museum; MAP: **19** P144 **B4**) across the road, whose main section occupies a disused but impressive Ashkenazi synagogue. It illustrates key religious and cultural Jewish customs through objects, videos and film fragments. It then tells the history of Amsterdam's Jewish community.

Examine VOC's Legacy   HISTORIC SITE

MAP: **20** P144 **A3**

Broach contentious history at the **Oost-Indisch Huis** *(uva.nl)*, an imposing red-and-white edifice built between 1551 and 1643 and attributed in part to city architect Hendrick de Keyser. It headquartered the Dutch East India Company (Vereenigde Oostindische Compagnie; VOC), trading spices, opium and more with Asia. The first ever share transactions were validated here.

The building is now part of the Universiteit van Amsterdam (UvA; University of Amsterdam) but visitors are welcome to look inside the *bewindhebberzaal*, the VOC's former boardroom, reconstructed in period grandeur in 1997. Closing in 2022 when the university recoiled from the apparent expression of pride in power and wealth while the 'suffering of exploited, enslaved Asians is invisible', it reopened as a part of a public programme of Decolonial Dialogues. A video narrative now includes the voices of descendants of those exploited calling for a fuller appreciation of the building's historical implications – a common thread gaining traction more widely as Amsterdam grapples with its past.

Preview the Architecture of Tomorrow

ARCHITECTURE

MAP: **21** P144 **D3**

Generally abbreviated **Arcam** *(arcam.nl/en/visit; adult/child €5/2.50/free)*, the Amsterdam Architecture Foundation inhabits a small but suitably distinctive building with metal curves and large glass walls, designed by Dutch architect René van Zuuk. Start a ¼-hour visit in the film booth for a six-minute *Future of Amsterdam* video looking at city-planning concepts from housing shortages to sustainability. Then peruse the one-wall timeline of architectural development this century. Open afternoons only. Check online listings for guided tours, usually in English on Sundays.

Hear Refugees' Stories

CRUISE

MAP: **22** P144 **D2**

Cruises along Amsterdam's waterways with **Rederij Lampedusa** *(rederijlampedusa.nl; 90-minute cruise €35)* are very special in that your pilot/guide will be telling you not just about Amsterdam but also of their personal experiences getting here. It's fascinating and moving in equal part, as they are all former asylum seekers with eye-opening, heartfelt perspectives. Some of the places your route passes have played a role in refugees' difficult process of regularisation. Tales might also weave in more generally how immigration has shaped Amsterdam and the city's history as a safe haven.

Both the 12m-long *Alhadj Djumaa* ('Mr Friday') and 6m-long

ICONIC ENTERTAINMENT VENUES

Muziekgebouw aan 't IJ

MAP: **23** P144 **D1**

Glass-and-steel concert venue, with an intimate jazz stage, **Bimhuis**. *muziekgebouw.nl*

Nationale Opera & Ballet

MAP: **24** P144 **A4**

Home to the Netherlands Opera and the National Ballet. *operaballet.nl*

CvA (Conservatorium van Amsterdam)

MAP: **25** P144 **C2**

The Netherlands' largest and most prestigious music academy; frequent student concerts. *conservatorium vanamsterdam.nl*

Amsterdams Marionetten Theater

MAP: **26** P144 **B3**

Endearing puppet theatre presenting fairy tales and Mozart operas. *marionettentheater.nl*

Kriterion

MAP: **27** P144 **C6**

Historic 1945 Resistance-founded arthouse cinema that began life as a student association. *kriterion.nl*

Hedir previously undertook perilous voyages bringing migrants across the Mediterranean to Lampedusa in Italy.

Booking ahead is essential. Trips depart beside the sustainable arts centre Mediamatic.

Best Places for...

€ Budget €€ Midrange €€€ Top End

See p144 for map of locations

Eating

Sandwiches

Frank's Smoke House €

28 E4

Salmon, mackerel, eel, goose, cheeses and much more, smoked on site and sold by weight or as sandwiches. *11am-6pm Tue-Sat, to 5pm Sun*

Sterk Staaltje €

29 A4

Gorgeous, luxury deli with a tantalising range of ready-to-eat treats, made-to-order sandwiches and bottled fresh juices. *8.30am-7pm Mon-Sat, 10am-7pm Sun*

TisFris €

30 A4

Split-levelled contemporary cafe that's handy for light lunches notably homemade soups, organically based salads and tasty open sandwiches.

Vegan and veggie options. *9am-7pm*

Barlotta €

31 G3

Causing a stir since 2024 for spot-on Mediterranean meals along with top-of-the-range charcuterie. *sandwiches noon-4pm, restaurant 5pm-midnight Tue-Sat*

Ice Cream

Bar Gelateria Tofani €

32 A3

Homemade Italian ice cream; deliciously tart lemon sorbet is an ideal cool-down during a hot summer stroll. *10am-1am*

IJscuypje Plantage €

33 D4

Handy for excellent creamy icecream as you exit the zoo. The growing IJscuypje chain is noted for using fresh, sometimes novel ingredients and flavours. *noon-9pm*

Light Bites

Droog €

34 A4

Hidden within a prize-winning design studio is a super-quaint mini garden and an upstairs cafe that's ideal for coffee or a light lunch. *10am-5pm*

In de Waag €€

35 A3

Fairly priced drinks and light meals, considering the location in and around Nieuwmarkt's defining 'castle' of a building. Candlelit interior at night. *11.30am-10pm*

Bakers & Roasters €€

36 D4

Great barista coffee made using Brazilian and Kiwi know-how. Wide-ranging international brunch menus are ethically sourced. *8.30am-3pm*

Box Sociaal €€

37 D5

Moreish brunch options from loaded bagels to signature aubergine

NIEUWMARKT, PLANTAGE & THE EASTERN ISLANDS

EXPLORE

parmigiana served on crispy fries. Good coffee, insistent musical beats. *9am-3.45pm*

Contemporary Cuisine

De Plantage
38 D5

Fresh, creative cuisine in an impressive 1870s zoo building. Terrace seats enjoy evening tree-lights and the whistled squawks of spoonbills. *10am-11pm*

Scheepskameel
39 D2

A cavernous, informal yet gastronomically excellent showcase for super-fresh ingredients beautifully cooked and matched with German wines. *6-9.30pm Tue-Sat*

Éénvistwéévis
40 D3

Locally famed for fresh seafood and fish served slowly but with love. The interior was totally reworked in a 2025 makeover. *6-10pm Wed-Sat*

Multicourse Menus

Gebr Hartering
41 C3

Founded by foodie brothers in a tiny wine-decor shophouse with canal views. Menus barely hint at the five- or seven-course adventure ahead. *6-9pm*

TestTafel
42 D2

Creative, highly experimental plant-based meals with many ingredients produced in Mediamatic's gardens and hydroponic greenhouses. *4-11pm Wed-Sat, kitchen 6-8pm*

Lastage
43 B2

Rogier van Dam's appealingly inviting gastronomic oasis is committed to sophisticated seasonal 'artisan' cuisine. *6.30-9pm Wed-Sun*

Dutch Cuisine

Rembrandt Corner
44 A4

Notable for offering classic Dutch *stamppot* (mashed veg/potato with sausage/meatball topping). *10am-10pm*

Fosco
45 H2

Come for the building's fascinating century-old history, stay for great beers, obliging service, upbeat music and well-made international street-food snacks. *5pm-midnight Mon-Thu, noon-1am Fri-Sun*

De Kop van Oost
46 G4

A modern canal-side brasserie near De Gooyer Windmill with imaginatively crafted sharing-style small-dish menus. *4-9.30pm Tue & Wed, 11am-9.30pm Thu-Sun*

Hemelse Modder
47 B3

Neat, simple decor leaves little to distract you from the entrancing flavours created in the chef's inventive multi-course menus. *6-10pm*

Asian Cuisine

Ayo Makan
48 E4

Satisfying point-and-pick Indonesian meals, served cold to take away or to eat at four window-stools. Even the smallest €10 options are very filling. *3.30-8.30pm*

Sea Palace
49 B2

Floating pagoda-style Chinese restaurant. Three floors are busy with locals and visitors, here for the great city views and extensive and delicious menu, including dim sum until 4pm. *noon-10pm*

De Japanner Strandeiland

50 H5

'Okinawa-style' beach cafe with bento box lunches, *izakaya*-style snacks and a full bar including various sakes. *noon-10pm Sat & Sun*

Krua Thai

51 A4

Officially certified as being truly authentic in its Thai flavours, though the spicy heat is reduced for European palates. Rice and tap water cost extra. *5.15-10pm*

Global Flavours

Tokoman

52 A3

Heavily automated take-away for wok dishes, Surinamese sandwiches and a wide variety of snack items. It's a few paces off Nieuwmarkt with a branch at Waterlooplein. *noon-9pm*

Sotto

53 D4

Scrumptious thin-crust pizza served in the historic former 'People's Union' coffeehouse beside the Entrepotdok gateway arch. Orders by QR code. *5-10pm Mon-Thu, noon-10pm Fri-Sun*

Cantina Caliente

54 D6

School chairs and distressed walls softened with cacti make a happy, informal spot for cocktails, Homeland beers and starter-size Mexican dishes. *noon-11pm*

Drinking

Cocktails

Rosalia's Menagerie

55 A3

Ring the doorbell to access this small, intimate but utterly exuberant drawing-room bar where creative tipples focus on Dutch heritage and seasonal botanicals. *6pm-1am*

HPS

56 C3

The low-lit, party vibe has none of the stuffiness of many cocktail bars. Barfolks really know their mixes and create some special novelties. *6pm-late*

Cafe Cuba

57 A3

Laid-back cocktail cavern that feels like you're on a Caribbean beach minus the sand...especially after sampling eight varieties of mojito. *noon-1am*

LuminAir

58 B2

Large, contemporary glass-walled bar on the triangular rooftop of the DoubleTree Inn Hotel. Prize-winning mixologists create a suave palette of colours and flavours. *noon-late*

Outdoor Terraces

Hannekes Boom

59 D2

Sprawling waterside cafe built from recycled materials with huge bench-tabled beer garden beneath colourful lights. Winter fires inside. Late-night dancing possible. *11pm-late*

De Sluyswacht

60 B4

Occupies a wonderfully wonky 1695 lock-keeper's house. Interiors are sparse and occasionally raucous. Canal-side terrace is a charmer. *noon-late*

Café de Doelen

61 A4

Textbook *bruin café* (traditional pub) dating back to 1895. The most prized outdoor terrace tables lie across the street at the canal-side. *11am-late*

Gollem an het Water

 62 E4

Mini-chain of beer lovers' bars. Hard to beat for brew choice; try 'Precious' semi-cloudy IPA. Board games and TV sports upstairs. *4-11.30pm*

Bruin Cafés

Café Scharrebier

63 C3

This unreconstructed locals' brown bar (traditional pub), with 10 great-value Benelux beers on tap, is a fine down-market alternative to nearby De Druif (p149). *11am-late*

Lokaal 't Loosje

64 A3

Nieuwmarkt's cult Art Nouveau *café* retains pictorial wall tiling from its days as a horse-tram waiting room. Excellent beer choice, heated terrace. *8am-1am*

Café Eik en Linde

65 C5

Super-friendly locals' bar where knowledgeable staff obligingly match beer newbies with a brew they're likely to enjoy. *11am-late Mon-Fri, 2pm-2am Sat*

De Groene Olifant

66 E5

Nineteenth-century elegance meets modern Bohemian with tiled floors, dark bentwood chairs and leaf-print wallpaper. Tram routes 7 and 14 meet outside. *3pm-1am*

Shopping

Music & Photography

Zwart Goud

67 B2

Sip super-strong coffee while perusing a subterranean vinyl record selection. 90-minute DJ-ing lessons available. *9am-6pm Mon-Fri, 10am-6pm Sat*

Analogue

68 B3

Old-school cameras including Polaroids plus photo development and scanning. It hosts guided photowalks. *10am-5pm Mon-Sat*

Gifts & Souvenirs

Jacob Hooy & Co

69 A3

Photogenic 1743 pharmacy with teas, sweets, medicinal herbs, homeopathic remedies and natural cosmetics. *10am-6pm Mon-Fri, to 5pm Sat*

DSign

70 A4

Colourful accoutrements, notably by-Lin's tulip bags and purses, which come in a whole rainbow of colour varieties. *10am-7pm*

Knuffels

71 A4

Toy shop with plenty of *knuffels* (soft cuddly toys), puppets and jigsaw puzzles. *10.30am-8pm*

See p169
for eating and
drinking listings

Explore

Researched by
Barbara Woolsey &
Catherine Le Nevez

Amsterdam Noord

The fun of Noord starts right on the ferry – the free, five-minute cruise across the IJ from central Amsterdam is a sightseeing experience in its own right. The neighbourhood, a previously neglected area (controversially, until recently, often not considered part of Amsterdam), which has been reinvented as one of the city's most happening neighbourhoods. It encompasses ex-industrial areas and hangars covered in street art – though changing winds see shiny condominiums and commercial spaces edge out obscure, alternative venues and some once-treasured haunts. It's all minutes away from fields, horses and the odd windmill that are perfect for exploring on the back of a bike.

Getting Around

 Ferry

Free 24-hour passenger/bicycle ferries link the rest of the city with Noord every 10 to 15 minutes. Key routes are NDSM to/from Centraal Station and Pontsteiger (Houthaven); and Buiksloterweg to/from Centraal. Between Buiksloterweg and NDSM, it's often quicker to return and change ferries at Centraal than wait for buses.

 Metro

The north–south line 52 links Amsterdam Zuid in the south with Noorderpark and Noord stations via Amsterdam Centraal Station.

 **Cycling**

A bike is near-essential for exploring spread-out Noord.

IJ Hallen (p165)
NICHON GLERUM, VIA IJ HALLEN

★

THE BEST

VIEWS
A'DAM Tower (p164)

STREET ART SPECTACLE
Straat (p165)

ARTIST STUDIOS
NDSM Loods (p165)

FLEA MARKET
IJ Hallen (p165)

FILM MUSEUM
Eye Filmmuseum (p168)

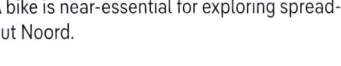

A B C D

1

s118

Metaalbewerkerweg

Ms van Remsdijkweg

NDSM

Nevenitaweg

NDSM-plein

Klaprozenweg

Papaverweg

2

3

Grasweg

Distelweg

Korte Papaverweg

4

8

Het IJ

Asterweg

Chrysantenstraat

NXT Museum 2

Distelweg

4

13

Heimansweg

Grasweg

Sesanstelindaan

Van der Pekstraat

Randdorfsde

Meadonweg

5

Westerdoksdijk

Ijpromenade

Badhuiskade

Berg Van Bod

Buiksloterweg

Eye Filmmuseum 1

6

A'DAM Tower

Buiksloterweg
Ferry Terminal

Ijplein Ferry
Terminal

IJ Tunnel

A B C D

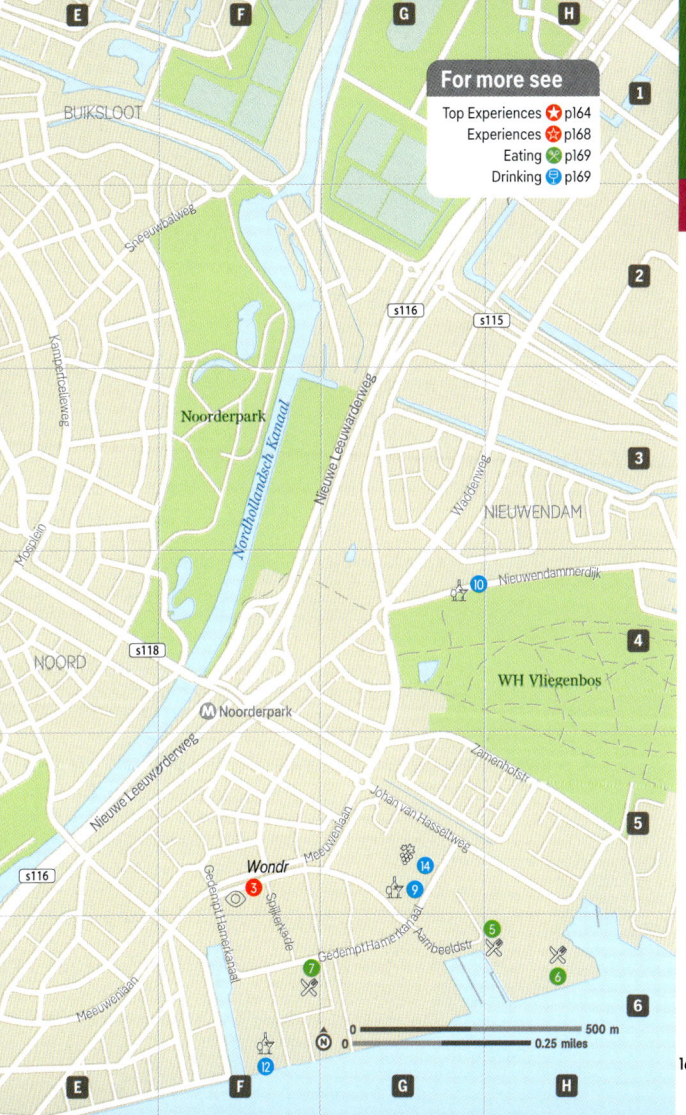

For more see

Top Experiences ⭐ p164
Experiences ✸ p168
Eating ✕ p169
Drinking 🍷 p169

BUIKSLOOT

Sneeuwbalweg

Noorderpark

Nordhollandsch Kanaal

Nieuwe Leeuwarderweg

Kamperfoelieweg

Mosplein

s116

s115

NIEUWENDAM

Waddenweg

Nieuwendammerdijk

10

WH Vliegenbos

NOORD

s118

Ⓜ Noorderpark

Nieuwe Leeuwarderweg

Zamenhofstr

Johan van Hasseltweg

Meeuwenlaan

Wondr

3

Gedempt Hamerkanaal

Spijkerkade

14

9

Gedempt Hamerkanaal

Aambeeldstr

5

7

6

Meeuwenlaan

12

500 m

0

0.25 miles

⭐ **TOP EXPERIENCE**

A'DAM Tower

Highrise A'DAM Tower was built in 1971 and named the 'Overhoeks' (Diagonal) because of its angle to the rest of the building. Used as the Royal Dutch Shell oil company offices, it's now a multi-venue extravaganza, with a 360-degree viewing platform on its 100m-high rooftop.

MAP P162 **C6**

PLANNING TIP
There's a €2 discount for lookout tickets if you book them online but you can also buy them on site. Combination tickets are available for A'DAM Tower's various attractions.

Scan this QR code for full opening hours and to book lookout tickets.

Sky Deck

The 22-storey A'DAM Tower provides a stark contrast to Amsterdam's relatively low-rise cityscape. The trippy lift, with a mesmerising light show overhead, whisks you up 100m in 20 seconds to the sky deck for sweeping views in all directions – complete with interactive binoculars and super-size cushions for lounging in fine weather. Lookout tickets include a free audio guide.

A giant swing – Europe's highest – kicks out over the edge for those who have a head for heights (*€7.50 per person*). Don't worry – you're strapped in.

You can also add on an 'Amsterdam VR Ride' (*€7.50*), taking you on a wild simulated roller-coaster ride through the historic city.

Drink, Dine & Dance

On the 20th floor, swish bar and nightclub **Madam** has stunning, floor-to-ceiling windows and DJ sets on Friday and Saturday nights from 10pm to 5am to hit Amsterdam's highest dancefloor. A floor below, the revolving restaurant **Moon** pairs 360-degree panoramas (at a one-revolution-an-hour pace) with modern Dutch, seasonally influenced tasting menus (book well ahead).

In the basement, **Shelter** goes deep as one of Europe's best nightclubs for underground house and techno. A raw, industrial, 700-person-capacity space runs to 7am on weekends thanks to a 24/7 licence.

NDSM

The NDSM former shipbuilding yard was an important industrial area that fell out of use from the 1980s, before squatters filled the void. Today it has numerous cool waterside restaurants, a street-art museum, a hangar full of artists' studios and huge monthly IJ Hallen flea market.

MAP P162 **A1**

Art City

Named for the Nederlandsche Dok en Scheepsbouw Maatschappij (the Netherlands Dock & Shipbuilding Company, which operated here from 1946–79), the shipyard turned edgy arts community retains its raw vibe despite encroaching gentrification and pressure from developers. At massive warehouse **NDSM Loods** (*ndsmloods.nl),* over 80 studios have some 250 artists working in the NDSM *broedplaats* (breeding ground). Huge artworks hang from rafters; up scaffolding-like stairs, **NDSM Fuse** (*ndsm -fuse.eu; by donation)* opens Thursday to Sunday.

NDSM equates to an open-air art museum. Graffiti around here is legally regulated and tolerated, so new works appear regularly. NDSM also harbours the world's largest museum for graffiti and street art, **Straat** (*straatmuseum.com; adult/child €19.50/ free),* where more than 150 works spread across 8000 sq metres.

Flea Market

Europe's largest flea market **IJ Hallen** (*ijhallen. nl; adult/child €6/2.50)* takes place one weekend a month (Saturdays and Sundays). Hundreds of stalls selling vintage clothes, antiques, vinyl, art and much more set up outside from April to September, and move into two NDSM warehouses from October to March.

PLANNING TIP
Festivals at NDSM include Easter weekend's three-day electronic music/arts festival **DGTL** (*dgtl-festival.com),* which also hosts a programme during October's **Amsterdam Dance Event** (ADE); check NDSM's website for other events.

Scan this QR code for full opening hours and more information.

🚲 **CYCLING TOUR**

Cycle Amsterdam Noord

Escaping to the countryside is surprisingly easy in Noord. From Centraal Station, hopping off the F3 Ferry at Buiksloterweg with your bike puts you right by the Noordhollandsch Kanaal. This ride follows the canal through a sprawling park, past a classic windmill and into a shaded forest, to see impressive 19th-century *sluices* (locks) and a fabulous fresh produce market.

START	END	LENGTH
Noordhollandsch Kanaal	Landmarkt	8.7km; 2½hr

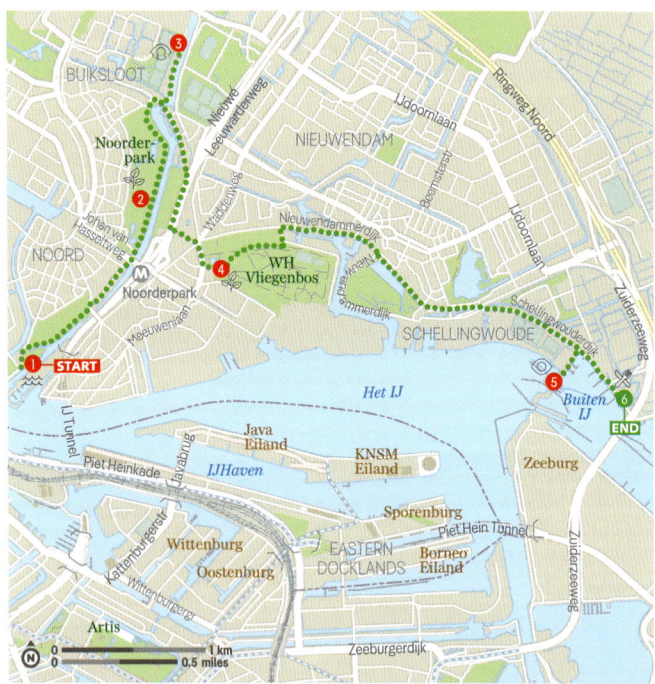

① Mighty Canal

Built between 1819 and 1824 to allow large ocean-going vessels to bypass the shallow Zuiderzee, the **Noordhollandsch Kanaal** was the longest, deepest and widest canal in the world when it opened. The mighty waterway stretches 79km from the IJ all the way to Den Helder in Noord-Holland (North Holland).

② Green Space

Straddling both sides of the Noordhollandsch Kanaal, the lawns, woodland and formal rose gardens of the rambling, 41-hectare **Noorderpark** are home to regular events like outdoor art classes and cinema screenings, and host festivals including September's Noorderpark Festival with food trucks and live music.

③ Traditional Windmill

Dating from 1792, national monument **Krijtmolen d'Admiraal** ('chalkmill d'Admiraal') still mills chalk that was used over the years by artists such as Piet Mondrian. Even when it's not open inside, seeing its sails spinning beside the canal is a quintessential Dutch scene.

④ Wildlife Haven

Planted from 1912, Noord's 20-hectare forest **WH Vliegenbos** is Amsterdam's oldest, with elm, ash and black alder trees and birdlife including woodpeckers, kingfishers, falcons and blackbirds. Walking and cycling trails weave through the greenery and past ponds and waterways.

⑤ River Locks

A monumental feat of 19th-century engineering to prevent excess saltwater flowing from the IJ into the IJsselmeer and regulate the canal's water levels, the 1870-opened **Oranjesluizen locks** are used by 120,000 vessels every year. Fish passages installed in 2019 allow species like perch, sturgeon and pike to pass through during their migrations. Awesome views from here take in the skyline of the Eastern Islands beyond.

⑥ Covered Market

Airy farm-shop-style covered market **Landmarkt** is piled high with fresh fruit and vegetables, locally caught seafood delivered by boat, Dutch cheeses and artisan breads. There's a great cafe-restaurant and outdoor seating that feels immersed in countryside. From Landmarkt, you can cycle 5km west to return to the ferry; take the Zuiderzeeweg south across the IJ to the Eastern Islands; or, if you're not ready to return to the city just yet, ride east into picturesque Waterland.

EXPERIENCES

See Amsterdam's Eye-Conic Film Museum
MUSEUM, CINEMA

MAP: **1** P162 **C6**

On the riverbanks of the IJ (also pronounced 'eye'), the modernist angular white **Eye Filmmuseum** (*eyefilm.nl; film adult/child €13.50/€8; exhibition adult/child €21/free*) peers over the city. Its permanent exhibition, *What is Film?*, lets you see how the earliest cameras worked, insert yourself into a film using green-screen technology, or make your own animated movie. Virtual reality focuses on the future, and all these eras come together in an installation called Film Catcher where an AI-powered, image-based search allows you to call up film clips from a collection of over 60,000 in mere seconds.

Eye's four state-of-the-art cinemas screen everything from Tinsel Town's latest blockbusters to experimental arthouse in original version; one has an organ for live sound effects, another boasts retractable seating. Analogue films also twinkle anew here with digital restoration.

Check Out the Nexus of Art & Tech
MUSEUM

MAP: **2** P162 **C4**

In a 1400-sq-metre warehouse space, 'new media art' museum **NXT Museum** (*nxtmuseum.com; adult/child from €19.50/13.50*) is a radical departure from traditional art forms. Artists, scientists, sound engineers, coders and designers collaborate to create immersive digital experiences of light, sound and movement using cutting-edge tech such as robotics, facial recognition, AI and VR. Large-scale, multisensory installations explore themes such as virtual worlds and digital identity through exhibits like evolving data sculptures.

Enter the Ballpit
ARTS CENTRE

MAP: **3** P162 **F5**

An interactive art experience in a gigantic pastel-pink building, play space **Wondr** (*wondrexperience. com; adult/child €26/18*) is an Instagram post brought to life. There are pits for swimming in Styrofoam 'marshmallows' and coloured balls, a pink bouncy castle, confetti room, art installations packed with teddies and more. Immersive pop-up exhibitions plop you right into Barbie Land and hanging with SpongeBob in Bikini Bottom. Outside, a 'beach' complete with pink sand has a cocktail bar and cafe.

LISTINGS

Best Places for...

ⓔ Budget   ⓔⓔ Midrange   ⓔⓔⓔ Top End

See p162 for map of locations

Eating

Contemporary Cuisine

Cornerstore ⓔⓔ
4 D3

Rustic interiors from the rafters to the vinyl DJ's booth; Asian-influenced warm and cold plates, plus seafood. *6.30pm-1am Wed & Thu, from 6pm Fri & Sat, 1.30-10pm Sun*

Barracuda ⓔⓔⓔ
5 H6

A fan favourite since opening in 2024, industrial-chic warehouse serving small seafood plates. Make a reservation to get prime seating on the sunny terrace. *5-11pm Mon-Thu, to 1am Fri, 12.30pm-1am Sat, to 10pm Sun*

Garage Dining

Hotel de Goudfazant ⓔⓔ
6 H6

In a cavernous former garage, still raw and industrial, with cars parked inside. Chefs cook up a French-influenced storm in the open kitchen. (There is no hotel, FYI, except in name.) *6pm-midnight Tue-Sun*

Euro Pizza ⓔⓔ
7 F6

Cult former garage, known for its sourdough pizza menu with locally sourced toppings paired with natural wines. *6-11pm, from 1pm Fri & Sat, 1-10pm Sun*

Eco-Friendly Eating

Cafe de Ceuvel ⓔⓔ
8 D3

Off-grid waterside spot on the cutting edge of sustainability – from recycled materials to an all-vegan menu. *noon-11pm Tue, Wed & Sun, to midnight Thu, to 1am Fri & Sat*

Drinking

Cafe-Bars

Skatecafe
9 G5

Expansive, warehouse-like cafe-restaurant with an indoor skate ramp and DJ line-ups. *3pm-1am Thu, to 3am Fri & Sat*

Café 't Sluisje
10 G4

Historic *bruin café* (traditional pub) overlooking a *sluis* (lock). Very pretty spot, inviting terrace.

11am-midnight Tue-Thu & Sun, to 1am Fri & Sat

Pllek
11 A2

Come for afternoon beer on the waterfront, stay for live DJs and dance parties pumping late. *9.30am-1am, to 3am Fri & Sat*

Artisanal Drinks

Lowlander
12 F6

Plant-filled former warehouse on the waterfront, with a sun-soaked, south-facing terrace that brews its own botanical beers. *11am-midnight, to 1am Thu-Sat*

Walhalla Taproom
13 C4

Relaxed microbrewery for unpretentious, delicious pours. *4pm-midnight Thu & Fri, from 2pm Sat, 2-9pm Sun*

Chateau Amsterdam
14 G5

The Netherlands' first urban winery. Grapes from around Europe become vino on site. Hit the terrace, tour the solar-powered production facility. *5pm-midnight Wed-Fri, from 2pm Sat, to 7pm Sun*

EXPLORE

LEIDEN & THE BOLLENSTREEK

Leiden & the Bollenstreek

Threaded by canals lined by 17th-century buildings, Rembrandt's birthplace, Leiden, is home to the Netherlands' oldest, most prestigious university and a cache of museums within walking distance of each other. It's a grand gateway to the Bollenstreek bulb fields and Keukenhof's magnificent spring gardens.

GETTING THERE
Leiden is 43km southwest of Amsterdam, served by NS trains (from €11.30; 37 minutes). 'KeukenhofBuzz' shuttle buses from Amsterdam, Schiphol Airport, Leiden or Haarlem are included in combitickets with Keukenhof admission.

Scan this QR code for more information about Leiden and its surrounds.

Fine Arts

Leiden's standout **Museum De Lakenhal** (*laken hal.nl; adult/child €16/free*), closed Monday, occupies a 1640-built premises (a former cloth warehouse) where it displays its exceptional permanent collection. Masterpieces include *The Spectacles Pedlar* by the city's native son Rembrandt, *The Astronomer* by Gerrit Dou (Rembrandt's first student), *Playing Couple* by Jan Steen, and *The Last Judgement* by Lucas van Leyden.

The 17th-century house where Rembrandt learned his craft between 1606 and 1630, now the **Young Rembrandt Studio** (*adult/child €2.50/free*), closed Mondays, is along the 4.5km **Rembrandt Route**.

Historic University

The Netherlands' oldest university, **Universiteit Leiden** (*universiteitleiden.nl*), was a gift to Leiden from William the Silent in 1575 for withstanding two Spanish sieges in 1573 and 1574. Collections include the impressive science- and medicine-focused **Rijksmuseum Boerhaave** (*rijksmuseumboerhaa ve.nl; adult/child €16.50/6*); the **Rijksmuseum van Oudheden** (*rmo.nl; adult/child €14/free*), with Greek, Etruscan, Roman and Egyptian artefacts; and the national research institute for biodiversity, **Naturalis Biodiversity Center** (pictured; *naturalis. nl; adult/child €18/free*), housing Europe's oldest T-Rex skeleton.

SIMONE BOTH

Founded by the university in 1590, **Hortus Botanicus Leiden** *(hortusleiden.nl; adult/child €16.50/4.50)* is one of Europe's oldest botanical gardens. Admission often includes exhibitions at its 1633-founded **Oude Sterrewacht** (Old Observatory).

Bulb Fields & Blooms

Around Leiden, the flower fields of the Bollenstreek (Bulb Region) are ablaze with colourful tulips, jonquils, daffodils and hyacinths in spring (around mid-March to mid-May), and blooms such as dahlias, asters and sunflowers in late summer (mid-August to mid-October). Cycling is glorious; bring wheels from Amsterdam or rent them in Leiden and its surrounds.

In tulip season, the Bollenstreek's biggest draw is **Keukenhof** *(keukenhof.nl; adult/child €21/9, combi-ticket from RAI €37/17.50, Haarlem, Schiphol or Leiden €32/15)*, 18km north of Leiden in Lisse. More than 7 million bulbs incorporating over 800 varieties of tulips, planted by hand every autumn, burst into bloom during Keukenhof's two-month-long opening season.

KEUKENHOF PLANNING

Keukenhof opens from mid-March to mid-May. Prebook timeslot entry tickets (valid until the park closes). Tickets are available online from mid-November. Bring extra layers, waterproof footwear, a rain jacket and/or umbrella.

Amsterdam Toolkit

Amsterdam's canals

Family Travel

Amsterdam is one of Europe's most kid-friendly cities. Virtually all quarters of the city are fair game for the younger set, there are parks and playgrounds galore, and sights and activities geared especially for kids.

Admission Prices

Most museums and attractions in Amsterdam have free entrance for babies and/or toddlers and reduced prices for children. However, the exact ages at which these cut off varies. Many places are free for those under six, sometimes 18; others offer child discounts for under 12s, and student discounts for older children.

TRAVEL LIGHT

Save on airline baggage fees by renting equipment such as strollers, baby carriers and highchairs on arrival in Amsterdam. Organisations such as Babyrent *(babyrent.com)* and Babonbo *(babonbo.com)* can deliver items to locations including Schiphol Airport or your hotel.

Public Transport

Children under four ride for free in Amsterdam. For kids aged four to 11, the best deal is often a €5 GVB children's day pass. These need to be purchased physically from a GVB service point. If using a debit card to tap in and out, the full fare will be charged. A family might find a GVB five-person 'Group Day Pass' (€26) cost effective.

Children's Cinema

Many cinemas show kids' films; the **Eye Filmmuseum** (p168) has Sunday Cinemini sessions for children under seven.

Pedal Power

Most bike-rental shops hire bikes with baby or child seats, cargo bikes and children's bikes, plus helmets (or BYO).

Dining with Kids

Some cafes have *kindermaaltijden* (kids' menus) while many *borrel* (snack) options include items like *kroketten* (croquettes) that children might favour anyway. You might look for a *pannenkoekenhuis* serving thin, oversized Dutch pancakes; *poffertjes* (mini pancakes; pictured) are a popular market-stall treat.

Accommodation

Amsterdam's charming accommodation doesn't come cheap and space is at a premium – reserve as far ahead as possible year-round.

Where to Stay if You Love...

 Centuries-old canal houses, abundant bars & entertainment

Medieval Centre & the Red Light District (p33) At the beating heart of sights, nightlife, theatres and transport; some parts can be noisy, touristy and seedy.

HOW MUCH FOR A NIGHT IN

Hostel dorm bed
€25–80

Midrange hotel
from €100

Top-end hotel
from €180

OUR PICK

★

We Love to Stay in...

Vondelpark, Oud-West & Oud-Zuid (p95)

Close to central Amsterdam but far enough away to find peace and quiet, this neighbourhood is fantastic for blockbuster museums, parks and neighbourhood strolls. Oud-Zuid's genteel, leafy streets around the Vondelpark are walking distance to Museumplein; increasingly happening Oud-West's backstreets are liveliest around cultural centre De Hallen.

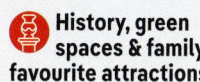 **History, green spaces & family-favourite attractions**

Nieuwmarkt, Plantage & the Eastern Islands (p143) Lower-key Nieuwmarkt is near the action. Plantage properties sit amid peaceful greenery. Eastern Islands addresses can be further flung.

Atmospheric streetscapes, markets & boutique shopping

Jordaan & the Western Canal Ring (p53) Charming canals, boutiques, *bruin cafés* and markets are close to popular sights, West's creative spaces are easily reached.

Famous nightlife venues & unique museums

Southern Canal Ring (p79) Central location handy for canal-house museums and restaurants. Can be loud, crowded and touristy, especially around nightlife hubs Leidseplein and Rembrandtplein.

Street art & reimagined industrial spaces

Amsterdam Noord (p161) Just across the IJ River, Noord has a burgeoning drinking, dining and creative scene, and some truly unique places to stay. Transport is limited in some areas.

175

Food, Drink & Nightlife

🐟 Allergies & Intolerances

Travellers with allergies and intolerances will generally have no problems in and around Amsterdam (an exception is high-end establishments offering 'surprise', no-choice menus); check when you book and communicate your requirements clearly with staff to be sure.

HOW TO SAY

I'm allergic to... *Ik ben allergisch voor...*

...peanuts *...pinda's*

...nuts *...noten*

...seafood *...zeevruchten*

...eggs *...eieren*

...milk *...melk*

...gluten *...gluten*

> **?**
> **HOW TO ASK...**
> **Is this gluten-free?**
> *Is dit glutenvrij?*
> **Does this contain nuts?**
> *Zitten hier noten in?*
> **Is there a vegan option?**
> *Is er een veganistische optie?*

COFFEESHOPS VS CAFÉS

In Amsterdam, it's crucial to know the difference between a *coffeeshop* (marijuana-smoking cafe), a *koffiehuis* (coffee shop), as in a specialist espresso bar serving barista-made coffee, and a *café* (pub). A *coffeeshop* may serve coffee (never alcohol), but its focus is cannabis and hash. Smoking (any substance) is banned by law in *cafés*.

Vegetarians & Vegans

As part of its commitment to sustainability, plant-based dining is increasingly prevalent in Amsterdam, where flexitarian, vegetarian or vegan dining is common. Vegetarians and vegans will find options in all price categories. There are numerous cafes and restaurants that are exclusively vegetarian or completely vegan; others invariably have options available.

Pay the Bill

At many restaurants, staff will ask upfront if you would like separate bills (*aparte rekening*) or one (*één rekening*). Requesting separate bills from the outset considerably expedites settling up later.

After your meal, you can ask for '*De rekening alstublieft.*' ('The bill please.')

Tipping is customary, but not obligatory. Check the bill to see if the service charge is already included. Typically, people round up the bill or leave a small tip of around 5%; a 10% tip is considered generous. State the amount you want to pay, including the tip, as you hand your payment to your server.

PRICE RANGES

The following price categories refer to the cost of a main course:

€ less than €12
€€ €12–25
€€€ over €25

OPENING HOURS

Bakeries 8am–5pm
Restaurants Lunch 11am–2.30pm, dinner 6–10pm
Cafés/Bars noon–1am Sunday to Thursday, to 3am Friday and Saturday

Going Out

Cafés Amsterdam is a *café* (pub) society, with more than 1100. They're relaxed places to hang out for hours; many have outside terraces. Most serve food as well.

Bruin cafés (brown cafes; traditional drinking establishments, named for their dark interiors). An Amsterdam treasure, providing visitors with a nirvana of *gezelligheid* (conviviality, cosiness).

Borrel Literally meaning 'drink', socially, borrel is an informal gathering for drinks, invariably with some *borrelhapjes* (bar snacks) such as *bitterballen* (small croquettes).

Beer Clear, crisp lager (or Pilsner), beer is served cool and topped by a head of froth. *Een bier* or *een pils* will get you a normal glass; *een fluitje* is a tall, thin glass – perfect for refills.

Jenever (traditional Dutch gin). Made from juniper berries and drunk chilled. A *kopstoot* (head butt), is a glass of *jenever* with a chaser of beer.

Entertainment Venues and festivals are plentiful. Many live-music stages resist being confined to one genre.

HOW MUCH FOR A

Flat white coffee
€4

25cl glass of standard lager
€3.20–4

33cl glass of craft beer
€5.50–7

Lunchtime soup
€8

Sit-down pizza
€16–22

Three-course meal at a family restaurant
€59–89

Tasting menu with wine at a Michelin-starred restaurant
€250–400

LGBTIQ+ Travellers

To call Amsterdam a queer capital doesn't fully express just how welcoming and open the scene is throughout the city.

Amsterdam's LGBTIQ+ Scene

Historically tolerant, the Netherlands was the first country to legalise same-sex marriage (in 2001), and in 2025 it was rated by A3M as the third-safest place in the world for LGBTIQ+ travellers.

These days the main concentration of gay bars is in the Southern Canal Ring towards the western end of **Reguliersdwarsstraat** (*reguliers.net/english .php*). There's a street-party atmosphere on summer nights. Numerous venues are located in the surrounding streets.

Busy Warmoesstraat in the Red Light District, once a major hotspot, now hosts just a couple of infamous, kink-filled leather and fetish bars: ring doorbells to enter. There are laidback alternatives nearby at the upper end of the Zeedijk, notably **Café 't Mandje** (*cafetmandje.amsterdam*), which first became a gay bar in 1927.

OUR PICKS

Festivals

Pride Amsterdam *(pride.amsterdam; late-Jul to early Aug)* One of the world's major LGBTIQ+ celebrations, which features the world's only waterborne Pride parade on the first Saturday of August.

Roze Filmdagen *(rozefilmdagen.nl)* LGBTIQ+ film festival that's mostly held in March though there are also some summer screenings.

TIJGERTJE SPORTS CLUB

Tijgertje (*tijgertje.nl*) started out as a self-defence group but is now is an LGBTIQ+ general sports club where friends meet for fitness, swimming, basketball etc.

QUEER STORYTELLER TOURS

Queer Storyteller's Henk leads two-hour walking tours at 11am most Saturdays explaining Amsterdam's LGBTIQ+ history spanning 750 years.

Resources

● **gayamsterdam.com** lists hotels, shops and clubs, and provides maps.

● **pinkpoint.nl** is a one-stop-shop with an information kiosk and souvenir shop on Westermarkt that can help with details of parties, events and social groups.

Health & Safe Travel

Amsterdam is a remarkably safe and manageable city, and if you use your common sense you should have no problems.

CANNABIS

Although marijuana is technically illegal, it's tolerated to the degree that 165 registered 'coffeeshops' in Amsterdam are allowed to sell up to 5g per person per day. Don't buy weed on the streets. Remember to finish or destroy any coffeeshop supplies before leaving town to avoid trouble at customs.

Health & Emergency Services

For minor health concerns, see a local *drogist* (chemist) or *apotheek* (pharmacy, to fill prescriptions). For more serious problems, go to the casualty ward of a *ziekenhuis* (hospital) or call 112.

The website *huisartsenpostenamsterdam.nl* can help you decide whether to call an ambulance or seek non-critical assistance via a family doctor *(huisart)* or general practice centre *(huisartsenpost)*. Amsterdam Tourist Doctors *(amsterdamtouristdoctors.nl)* are very familiar with foreign insurance systems. Mondzorg Poli *(mondzorgpoli.nl/en)* has a 24/7 dental service.

Tap Water
Tap water in Amsterdam and Netherlands-wide is clean, pleasant and safe to drink.

Pickpockets & Scams

Stay alert for pickpockets, especially in the Red Light District and Leidseplein areas where crowds of visitors make for easy targets. Also be mindful of your possessions around Centraal Station, Bloemenmarkt, and on busy trams. Beware of very occasional 'fake police officer' scams where a stranger demands to look through your possessions.

--- **BEWARE OF BIKES** ---

Never walk in bicycle lanes and always check carefully before you cross. Look both ways even on a one-way street!

QUICK INFO

Security
Use two bike locks (one should be attached to a fixed structure).

Safety
Avoid deserted streets in the Red Light District at night.

Canals
Be careful around canals; almost none have fences or barriers.

179

Responsible Travel

Follow these tips to leave a lighter footprint, support local businesses and have a positive impact on communities.

Embrace Sustainability Goals

Visitors can play a big part in supporting Amsterdam's sustainability goals. In 2024, the Dutch capital was ranked the world's most sustainable city in Arcadis Sustainable Cities Index. By 2050, the city aims to be completely climate-proof, and to have a fully circular economy, reusing, repairing and recycling renewable materials. Reducing your energy consumption, minimising food and packaging waste, and dining and shopping sustainably will all help.

Low-Impact Transport

Amsterdam's flat landscapes are perfect for walking and cycling. Trains and all new buses use green electricity and by 2030 all buses are required to be emission free.

FROM LEFT: CHINNAPONG/SHUTTERSTOCK, BORA BALBEY/ SHUTTERSTOCK, WR7/SHUTTERSTOCK

OUR PICK ★

Hortus Botanicus
A green haven for centuries, botanic garden **Hortus Botanicus'** (p151) Climate House was renovated in 2025 to become the world's first fully sustainable, CO$_2$-neutral public greenhouse.

Meaningful Visits

Museums, including the excellent **Wereldmuseum** (p136), illuminate diverse cultures and colonial legacies. Eye-opening tour alternatives include refugee-guided cruises with **Rederij Lampedusa** (p155). **Tours that Matter** (*toursthatmatter. com*) dives into subjects like freedom, innovation, colonialism and fair trade, diverse society, urban agriculture and sustainability on walking and cycling tours. Get involved by renting emission-free boats and equipment from **Canal Motorboats** (p67) and fish plastic out of the canals.

Resources

- **amsterdam.nl** Amsterdam's strategy for becoming a fully circular economy.
- **conscioushotels.com** Small boutique hotel group.
- **toogoodtogo.com** Otherwise-wasted food-bargains app.

TestTafel (p157) serves experimental gastronomic vegan dinners using vegetables from Mediamatic's urban garden and scientific hydroponics greenhouse. Charming Medieval Centre cafe **Gartine** (p47) and Oost's Michelin-starred greenhouse restaurant **De Kas** (p141) also grow their own produce.

Sustainable Shopping

For food supplies, try plastic-free, zero-waste **Little Plant Pantry** (p115). Or take your own bags to a *boerenmarkt* (farmers market) and support local producers. Sustainable fashion designs include sneakers from pineapple leather, grapes, cacti or plastic ocean waste from **Mercer** (p131); backpacks and tote bags from recycled plastic from **Property Of...**(p93); and recycled-denim jeans at **Denim City** (p115).

DRINKING FOUNTAINS

Reduce waste from single-use plastic bottles. Bring a reusable bottle and fill it at one of Amsterdam's 500 taps and fountains. Scan this QR code to find them.

Climate Change & Travel

It's impossible to ignore the impact we have when travelling; Lonely Planet urges all travellers to engage with their travel carbon footprint, which will mainly come from air travel. While there often isn't an alternative, travellers can look to minimise the number of flights they take, opt for newer aircrafts and use cleaner ground transport, such as trains. One proposed solution – purchasing carbon offsets – unfortunately does not cancel out the impact of individual flights. While most destinations will depend on air travel for the foreseeable future, for now, pursuing ground-based travel where possible is the best course of action.

The **UN Carbon Offset Calculator** shows how flying impacts a household's emissions.

The **ICAO's carbon emissions calculator** allows visitors to analyse the CO_2 generated by point-to-point journeys.

Accessible Travel

Transport

Public transport can present challenges due to crowding and variable slopes. Most buses are wheelchair accessible, as are metro stations. Trams are becoming more accessible as new equipment is added. Many lines have elevated stops for wheelchair users. The website of **GVB** (*gvb.nl*) denotes which stops are wheelchair accessible.

Accessible Museums

Most of Amsterdam's big-hitter attractions are well equipped, but wheelchair users can't fully explore antique houses such as the **Museum Rembrandthuis** (p146). At the **Anne Frank Huis** (p56), the secret annexe is similarly inaccessible but a VR alternative is available.

TAXIS

Brouwer (*taxibrouwer .nl/en/taxi-services/ wheelchair-taxi*) has a few mini-van taxis that are equipped with either ramps or lifts to allow two wheelchairs to be ridden aboard plus room for at least four additional passengers. Pre-booking is strongly recommended.

Accommodation

Newer hotels typically have accessible rooms. However, many smaller hotels and guesthouses in older buildings either lack elevators or still require guests to use some steps to front doors and between floors.

OUR PICK

Amsterdam's top sight, the **Rijksmuseum** (p98), is impressively equipped for visitors with disabilities. To avoid queues, visitors can complete a 'fast lane declaration' (downloadable on its website). All floors of the 19th-century building are accessible by lift, and bathrooms are suitably equipped. The museum has a range of specially adapted visiting options, including family tours for people with visual impairment, dementia or special needs, or tours in international sign language. Special sensory-friendly evening openings provide a quieter atmosphere.

MUSIC VENUES

Amsterdam's foremost concert halls (p155) – including the **Nationale Opera & Ballet**, **Concertgebouw**, **Muziekgebouw aan 't IJ** and jazz stage **Bimhuis** – are fully accessible with dedicated spaces for wheelchair users.

Resources

● **ableamsterdam.com/practical-information-1** Provides a useful roundup of observations on the realities of transport practicalities for those with accessibility worries.

Nuts & Bolts

Opening Hours

Museums 10am–5pm; some close Mondays, especially outside of summer months

Cafés (pubs) and bars noon–1am Sunday to Thursday, to 3am Friday and Saturday

General office hours 8.30am–5pm Monday to Friday

Restaurants 11.30am–2.30pm and 6–9.30pm

Shops 9am or 10am to 6pm; some close Sundays and Monday mornings. Later opening is common in tourist areas and on Thursdays.

Supermarkets 7am or 8am to 8pm and 10pm

Open
Open
Closed
Gesloten

Public Toilets

Public toilets aren't widespread; many people duck into a *café* (pub; ask first!) or department store. Check the city's municipal interactive map at *maps.amsterdam.nl/openbare_toiletten*. The app HogeNood (High Need; *hogenood.nu*) maps the nearest toilets based on your location, listing facilities in locations like fast-food stores and public buildings.

QUICK INFO

Time zone Central European Time (GMT/UTC +1 hr)
Country calling code +31
Emergency number 112
Population 934,000 (metro area 2.5 million)

ELECTRICITY

Standard European Type C or F, 230V/50Hz

Type F
230V/50Hz

Public Holidays

Nieuwjaarsdag (New Year's Day) 1 January

Goede Vrijdag (Good Friday) March/April

Eerste Paasdag (Easter Sunday) March/April

Tweede Paasdag (Easter Monday) March/April

Koningsdag (King's Day) 27 April, or 26 April if the 27th falls on a Sunday.

Dodenherdenking (Remembrance Day) 4 May (unofficial)

Bevrijdingsdag (Liberation Day) Officially a holiday every 5th year.

Hemelvaartsdag (Ascension Day) 40th day after Easter Sunday.

Eerste Pinksterdag (Whit Sunday; Pentecost) Seven weeks after Easter Sunday.

Tweede Pinksterdag (Whit Monday)

Eerste Kerstdag (Christmas Day) 25 December

Tweede Kerstdag (Boxing Day) 26 December

💬 ？ Language

Basics

Hello.
Dag./Hallo. *dakh/ha-loh*

Goodbye.
Dag. *dakh*

Yes.
Ja. *yaa*

No.
Nee. *ney*

Please. (pol)
Alstublieft. *al-stew-bleeft*

Please. (inf)
Alsjeblieft. *a-shuh-bleeft*

Thank you. (pol/inf)
Dank u/je. *dangk ew/yuh*

Excuse me.
Excuseer mij. *eks-kew-zeyr mey*

💬 Fast Phrases

Excuse me. **Excuseer mij.** *eks·kew·zeyr mey*

Sorry. **Sorry.** *so·ree*

Do you speak English? **Spreekt u Engels?** *spreykt ew eng·uhls*

I don't understand. **Ik begrijp het niet.** *ik buh·khreyp het neet*

Where's ...? **Waar is ...?** *waar is ...*

What's the address? **Wat is het adres?** *wat is het a·dres*

Can you please write it down? **Kunt u dat alstublieft opschrijven?** *kunt ew dat al·stew·bleeft op·skhrey·vuhn*

Can you show me (on the map)? **Kunt u het mij tonen (op de kaart)?** *kunt ew het mey toh·nuhn (op duh kaart)*

What time is it? **Hoe laat is het?** *hoo laat is het*

It's (10) o'clock. **Het is (tien) uur.** *het is (teen) ewr*

Half past (10). **Half (elf).** *half (elf)* (literally: half eleven)

am (morning). **'s ochtends.** *sokh·tuhns*

pm (afternoon). **'s middags.** *smi·dakhs*

pm (evening). **'s avonds.** *saa·vonts*

Help! **Help!** *help*

Leave me alone! **Laat me met rust!** *laat muh met rust*

I'm sick. **Ik ben ziek.** *ik ben zeek*

Call a doctor! **Bel een dokter!** *bel uhn dok·tuhr*

Call the police! **Bel de politie!** *bel duh poh·leet·see*

What would you recommend? **Wat kan u aanbevelen?** *wat kan ew aan·buh·vey·luhn*

Cheers! **Proost!** *prohst*

Delicious! **Heerlijk/Lekker!** *heyr·luhk/le·kuhr*

Numbers

 één *eyn*

 twee *twey*

 drie *dree*

 vier *veer*

 vijf *veyf*

Distinctive Sounds

The pronunciation of Dutch is fairly straightforward. Some vowel sounds are a bit trickier for English speakers as they have no equivalent in English. Most common are *eu* (nasal **eu**, similar to the French vowel sound in *heur*) and *ui* (**oey**, similar to the French vowel sound in *oeil*). For consonants, note that **kh** is a throaty sound, similar to the 'ch' in the Scottish loch, **r** is trilled and **zh** is pronounced as the 's' in 'pleasure'.

What's in a Name?

Dutch words in street names and on signs are often combined into a single long place name, which can be tricky for a foreigner to decipher (eg *Derde Leliedwarsstraat* means 'third lily-cross-street').

Hold Your Vowels

Most vowels have a long and a short version, which simply means that you hold vowels for a greater or lesser length of time. It's important to make the distinction between long and short versions, as they can distinguish meaning – eg *maan* means 'moon' but *man* means 'man'.

TOOLKIT

LANGUAGE

WHO SPEAKS DUTCH?

Dutch, along with its variants including Flemish (Vlaams) in Belgium and Afrikaans (in South Africa), is spoken by between 20 and 25 million people worldwide.

Signs

Ingang Entrance

Gesloten Closed

Open Open

Uitgang Exit

Toiletten Toilets

LOCAL TALK

Hey! **He daar!** *hey daar*
Great! **Fantastisch!** *fan·tas·tis*
Sure. **Natuurlijk.** *na·tewr·luhk*
Maybe. **Misschien.** *mi·skheen*
No way! **Geen sprake van!** *kheyn spraa·kuh van*
Go ahead! **Doe maar!** *doo maar*
Just a minute. **Een minuutje.** *uhn mee·new·chuh*
Just joking! **Grapje!** *khrap·yuh*
It's OK. **In orde.** *in or·duh*
No problem. **Geen probleem.** *kheyn proh·bleym*
All's OK! **Alles kits!** *a·luhs kits*

6 **zes** *zes*

7 **zeven** *zey·vuhn*

8 **acht** *akht*

9 **negen** *ney·khuhn*

10 **tien** *teen*

Index

Sights p000 Map pages **p000**

See also separate subindexes for:
- 🍴 **Eating p190**
- 🍷 **Drinking p190**
- 🛍 **Shopping p191**

Eating

Drinking

Send Us Your Feedback

We love to hear from travellers – your comments help make our books better. We read every word, and we guarantee that your feedback goes straight to the authors. Visit lonelyplanet.com/contact to submit your updates and suggestions.

Note: We may edit, reproduce and incorporate your comments in Lonely Planet products such as guidebooks, websites and digital products, so let us know if you are happy to have your name acknowledged. For a copy of our privacy policy visit lonelyplanet.com/legal.

Acknowledgements

Cover photograph: Nico Schrenk/Stills

Back photograph: Nafre/ Shutterstock

THIS BOOK

The 10th edition of Lonely Planet's Pocket Amsterdam guidebook was researched and written by Catherine Le Nevez, Mark Elliott and Barbara Woolsey. The previous edition was written by Catherine Le Nevez. This guidebook was produced by the following:

Destination Editor
Daniel Bolger

Coordinating Editor
Anita Isalska

Cartographer
Jennifer Johnston

Production Editor
Ursula O'Sullivan-Dale

Image Researcher
Madison Reid

Assisting Editors
Sofie Andersen, Melanie Dankel, Kate James, Holly Proctor

Cover Researchers
Beatriz Atunes, Fergal Condon

Thanks to Fergal Condon, Gwen Cotter, Sandie Kestell, Kellie Langdon

Although the authors and Lonely Planet have taken all reasonable care in preparing this book, we make no warranty about the accuracy or completeness of its content and, to the maximum extent permitted, disclaim all liability arising from its use.

Published by Lonely Planet Global Limited

CRN 554153

10th edition – Jun 2026

ISBN 978 1 83758 430 7

© Lonely Planet 2026

10 9 8 7 6 5 4 3 2 1

Printed in China

Shopping